# PRAISE FOR
## *BECOMING A GODLY HUSBAND*

Dr. Gil Stieglitz is a master at helping marriages thrive. Since meeting Dr. Gil in 2004, we have helped many couples try out the biblical principles in the Godly Husband book. These well-thought concepts actually work when you put them into practice. Would you like to have a thriving marriage? Dr. Gil's new book is a key to your future happiness. We recommend that you buy a copy today.

— REV. DR. ED & JANICE HIRD
Authors of *For Better, For Worse*

Let's face it! We men are fixers and look for and implement solutions to the problems presented to us—especially by our wives. This book is a must in your reference library. Keep it close at hand. It has the solutions to fix nearly every problem in your marriage.

— JUD BOIES
Author of *Goals, The Church Quiz*, and *What's for Dessert?*

What a gift of surprise I received from Dr. Gil to read this book. It is an honor to write a very important sharing from the bottom of my heart! This book is a wonderful reminder to all husbands to love their wives as a loving H.U.S.B.A.N.D.! As I was about to finish reading this book yesterday, I was in the airport in Taipei, Taiwan, waiting to go home after an eight days trip to Sabah. I was about to buy two bottles of Bordeaux wine, and suddenly I thought of Dr. Gil's words of Honor, Understanding, and Agreement. A red light turned on, and I thought my wife would not be happy if I purchased the two expensive bottles of wine and decided she would be happy to receive a bottle of Christine Dior perfume instead. So, instead of gratifying my own desire, I chose to follow Dr. Gil's teaching to purchase the Dior for my wife. The result was a happy ending when I arrived home! You really need to read this book and read it well so that you can receive lots of blessings and anointing to be a better husband!

— RT. REV. DR. SILAS NG
Chief Bishop
Anglican Mission in Canada

REVISED EDITION

# BECOMING A

# GODLY HUSBAND

## WHAT YOUR WIFE WISHES YOU KNEW ABOUT HER

**PTLB**

PRINCIPLES
TO LIVE BY

LIFE IS RELATIONSHIPS

## GIL STIEGLITZ

*Becoming a Godly Husband: What Your Wife Wishes You Knew about Her*
Copyright © Gil Stieglitz, 1991, 2003, 2023

Published by PTLB Publishing, P.O. Box 214, Roseville, CA, 95661. For more information about this book and the author, visit www.ptlb.com.

Revised edition, third printing.

ISBN:     978-1-952736-02-5 (print)
          978-1-952736-03-2 (ebook)
          978-1-952736-01-8 (audio)

Library of Congress Control Number: 2023905428

**Copyediting & Production by:**
Jennifer Edwards | jedwardsediting.net

**Cover Design by:**
Dave Eaton

**Cover Photography by:**
Michael Carlos

**Book Design & Typography by:**
Linné Garrett | 829DESIGN.com

**Author Photo by:**
Hannah White

# DEDICATION

---

This book is dedicated to my wonderful wife,

Dana Stieglitz.

It is only through submission to God's principles
that I have been able to love this beautiful woman
as she deserves to be loved.

◆

# CONTENTS

# FOREWORD

I've seen my share of marriages that were declared OVER, and yet they survived to thrive. I've seen many relationships that were "dead on arrival" when they arrived in the pastor's or therapist's office, and yet a resurrection occurred. The power of the testimony gives hope to the hopeless. I want you to hear my testimony: I believe men are the key to the future of marriage. Yes, I know marriage is a "two-way street," and yes, "It takes two to tango." But I also know the power that men have in marriage and culture. This book is written for our time and setting. This book was written for *you*.

Marriage and family stand as the foundation of culture. I personally believe the epidemic of fatherlessness and its effect on a myriad of social concerns is the number-one social challenge of our day. The breakdown of a healthy marriage culture precedes the fatherlessness epidemic and, therefore, stands at the root of our problems. Sadly, the reality of marriage health in the church community and in the general public is often very similar.

So what are we to do? I say we rebuild healthy marriages and families one household at a time. The book you hold in your hands (or are reading online or a video course!) is literally almost the "owner's manual" for building a healthy marriage, one that is life-giving for men and women and will create a strong foundation to build thriving families. Healthy marriages have the power to build healthy families that have the power to change neighborhoods, communities, and nations.

I have known Gil Stieglitz for almost twenty years. Gil is no recently minted expert. Gil is not merely a writer of words. Gil has been living these principles for his entire adult life. I know Gil and his wife, Dana. They are the real deal. What you are reading in this book is what Gil practices in his home, what he shares with men (and women!) in the seminars and classes he teaches, and what has brought healing and hope to thousands of marriages.

This book has the potential to start a revolution! Men who are willing to ask Jesus, "What would you have me do in my marriage?" will find answers in this book that will revolutionize their marriages, family, and their witness in the world. A revolution of men who love and serve their wives can change the course of families, communities, and our world. That is a revolution I am looking forward to experiencing!

But please wait. Before you read, may I ask you to do something? Would you stop and say a quick prayer, "Father God, will you give me an open heart and open ears to hear what you want me to say, do, or stop doing so that I can create a marriage that is pleasing to you?" That prayer is a "dangerous prayer" but one that can change your life. I'm believing that for you and your beloved. Now, go after it and become a godly husband!

DR. JOHN JACKSON
President, William Jessup University

www.drjohnjackson.com

# A NOTE TO HUSBANDS

"Husbands, love your wives, just as Christ also loved the church
and gave Himself up for her."

Ephesians 5:25 NASB

——&infin;——

**G**od has a plan for husbands—to love their wives as Christ loves His Church, as specified in Ephesians 5:25. But reading about it and doing it are two different things. God commands husbands to love their wives, which means that a husband is to meet her needs, pursue her soul, and please her. Most husbands have no idea how to do this, at least in the way she needs him to. This book grew out of the radical idea that God knows what wives need, and He gave us husbands instructions on how to build an amazing marriage by loving our wives. This basic idea has proven to be true. When we follow God's prescription, it usually results in a delightful, God-centered marriage.

Since this book was first published in 1991, I have had the honor of hearing how this material has helped save many marriages. I am deeply grateful for all the couples this book has helped in the past and look forward to how this updated version will continue to carry God's plan for husbands to thousands more.

Marriages come in all shapes and sizes—no two are alike. And every marriage exists in various stages of success or failure. But marriage principles that were true ages ago are still true today. They are the very principles God set forth in His Word, and they are unchanging. This book not only tells you "what" the principles are but "how" to make them work for you wherever you are in your marriage. I'm glad you're reading it and hope you'll take everything in it to heart.

A man came up to me with a well-worn copy of my book in his hands. He told me he had bought it at a bookstore, hoping to find a way to salvage his crumbling marriage. He just couldn't get a handle on why his wife wanted to leave him. He told me, very excitedly, that this book explained why his marriage was falling apart and what he needed to do to fix it. By practicing the principles in this book, his marriage turned around. He learned what he needed to do to *really* love his wife and did something about it.

I have watched this material inject new levels of joy and delight into relationships that had fallen into the "mundane" category. One of the original editors of this manuscript told me this book had challenged him to step up his game in his marriage. His new efforts were making a significant difference with his wife.

I've learned of husbands using this material to take their "good" marriages and propel them to new levels. One older woman confessed she had bought the book to help me out. She didn't really think her husband or her marriage needed anything—she was happy. But with tears streaming down her face, she told me, "It has made my wonderful husband even more amazing. He loves me with such a new level of tenderness and effectiveness. Thank you for clearly saying what God tells husbands to do in a way they can understand."

Let me say clearly that this godly-husband plan is not guaranteed to save your marriage, though it has saved many marriages. Sometimes, the marriage still tumbles to destruction because of selfishness, past wounds, and outside influences. Jesus calls this a result of a "hardness of heart" (Matthew 19:8).

This book describes what God wants husbands to do for their wives, whether it "works" or not. A man must often learn how to love his wife in these ways and then lovingly teach his wife what it means to love him.

Throughout the Scriptures, God instructs husbands to do seven things that demonstrate love for their wives. These seven concepts describe what most wives would agree it means to truly love them. Once you learn the concepts in this book, it will become clear that this is not typically how a man would describe what it means to love his wife. That's because this is *God's* wisdom on how to love a woman at the core of her being.

To help you remember these seven key ideas about becoming a godly husband, I made each one a part of the acrostic H.U.S.B.A.N.D. Memorize this acrostic to help you remember the specific actions that are critical to your marriage. I also suggest memorizing Ephesians 5:25, "Husbands, love your wives, just as Christ also loved the church and gave Himself up for her." This is the foundational scripture for these principles. You may also want to take the short quiz I've placed in **Appendix 1** to get a feel for where you are currently meeting her needs and where you may be falling short.

In each chapter, there are short exercises for you to practice. Only when you do what the scriptures say does the benefit come. Most husbands see positive results right away, while it may take some time for other marriages. Truly a man must commit to working through these principles constantly to get to the place where his wife feels authentically loved. (FYI, it took me four-and-a-half years of practice.)

If you want to engage this material visually, I invite you to take the online video course called "How to Be a Good and Godly Husband" on Udemy.com. Just scan the QR code below.

Take your time and make deliberate, positive steps forward day-by-day, year by year. You won't regret it. Do the hard work to become a godly husband.

— GIL STIEGLITZ

How to Be a Good and Godly Husband
Online course at Udemy.com

# WHAT YOUR WIFE WISHES YOU KNEW ABOUT HER
# H. U. S. B. A. N. D

---

## Honor:
Do you treat your wife better than anyone else in your life?

## Understanding:
Are you quick to apologize and learn everything about her?

## Security:
Do you provide the security she needs financially, mentally, spiritually, and physically?

## Building Unity:
Do you lead her towards wisdom and unity?
Make sure she is never the enemy.

## Agreement:
Do you know how to make decisions together without conflict?

## Nurture:
Do you know what nurtures her spirit, mind, body, and soul?

## Defender:
Do you protect her from what will derail or destroy her?

---

# INTRODUCTION

# PURSUING A
# TRANSFORMATIONAL MARRIAGE

---

It was a Tuesday afternoon when my phone rang. I had no idea that the results of this phone call would completely change my understanding of marriage. On the other end of the line was a middle-aged woman I'll call Tiffany. Sobbing, she was having troubles in her marriage and could barely get it out. I agreed to see her at the church, and she poured out her heart. Everyone assumed she and her husband, Derek, had a great marriage, but from Tiffany's point of view, it was awful and loveless. I listened to her story about what it was really like to live with her husband. I then asked her to rate her marriage on a scale of one to ten, with one being the worst and ten being the best. She gave her marriage a three. She was ready to leave.

"There is no point in continuing," she said.

I asked her several questions to understand how long the problem had been going on and then asked, "Do you think your husband knows your marriage is in trouble?"

"No," she said, "that's one of the problems. He's a complete jerk. He tries to get everyone to believe he is so wonderful, but at home, he is an ogre."

I thought it couldn't be as bad as she was saying, so for the next hour, I did everything I could to convince her to stay in her marriage. And she did everything she could to convince me that Derek was a jerk. After an hour, she was winning.

Out of pure desperation, I asked her if she would be willing to wait five weeks before she left Derek...as a favor to me. My question dumbfounded her. I explained that while it might not work for Derek, I was beginning a new class in two weeks just for husbands. Her husband had signed up for it. I gave her a quick overview of the class and asked her again if she would wait before she left. After some thought, she agreed to wait five weeks to see if I could do anything with him.

After the third week of the class, she walked into the church all decked out with a new dress, a new hairdo, and new jewelry. I thought, "Oh, no! She is hunting for her new husband!" But to the contrary, she began bragging to the other ladies about how wonderful her husband was treating her and how strong her marriage was becoming. This was a huge change in just five weeks! She even told some women that she wished they had a husband like hers. The course for husbands was working. Derek had only been exposed to three weeks of the class, and it was already turning his marriage around!

---

Every husband has the power to heal his marriage or destroy it. You can make your relationship a delight or a disaster. I know what you are thinking, *But what about her? What about how horribly she acts?* I've heard it all before. In a few cases, a wife is so selfish and so monstrous there is no hope. But in the vast majority of the cases, learning to do the things that communicate love for her can change everything. Husband, you have a powerful ability to create a wonderful relationship.

A transformational marriage is made up of a man and a woman who commits to meeting one another's relational needs consistently for life. It involves sacrifice and a love that is willing to meet one another's needs, pursue one another's souls, and please each other. What a man needs from his marriage is totally different than what his wife needs. Likewise, your wife is looking for completely different things than what you need from her. She is usually willing to meet your needs, but she also is expecting you to meet hers. I know what you are thinking, *She should go first.* This is not how God thinks about it. He says *you* should go first. When mankind needed saving and was wretched, sinful, and rebellious, who started loving first, God or mankind? God did by sending His Son Jesus Christ into the world to die for our sins and give us a way back to Him from our rebellion. You, the husband, should demonstrate that you love your wife first before you ask her to meet your needs.

I remember one husband I'll call Tom. I was explaining these principles to Tom, who sadly, wanted no part of this kind of marriage. In Tom's mind, his wife existed for his needs. He just assumed she wanted to make him happy and that his happiness was enough for her. He could not understand what was wrong with this one-sided marriage. Needless to say, Tom's marriage didn't last very long.

This type of marriage may have worked in the past, but it is not biblical. The only way Tom's type of marriage "works" is if the wife is economically dependent on her husband and she has nowhere else to go. But these days, women can get a good job and may not need their husband's help financially. So this one-way marriage of the past is out. Women are fleeing this type of marriage in droves. After all, why would they want to stay in a marriage where their needs are never even considered?

The one-way marriage is certainly not the marriage of the Scriptures. God tells husbands that in order to have a good and healthy marriage—a transformational marriage—they are to give themselves up to unfold the wonder of their wives—just as Christ is doing for the Church (Ephesians 5:25–28).

## God's Plan for Husbands

Scripture calls married men *husbands*—a word short for *husbandman*. In the ancient world, the husbandman was the gardener of the vineyard. He was responsible for making the vineyard produce the healthiest and most productive grapes each year. Likewise, in marriage, a man who becomes a husband is called upon to help his marriage thrive by tending to his wife so she can become the woman she is meant to be personally, maritally, in her family, professionally, and within her community (Proverbs 31:10–31). But too often husbands have been tricked by society into giving all their time, energy, and resources to work on their own selfish pursuits, and this leaves the core of their life relationally dead. As Benjamin Disraeli said, "No amount of public success can make up for failure in the home."[1]

If you accept the role as the husbandman, or gardener, then you will need to do whatever it takes to help your wife blossom and flourish. Whatever type of fertilizer she needs, you supply it; whatever amount of water she needs, you fill her up; whatever amount of sunlight she needs, you expose her to it; whatever type of protection from bugs, rodents, or birds she needs, the husbandman will provide it; whatever amount of weeding around the vines is needed, you make sure it gets done. The husbandman does not compare the amount of work he has to do with another gardener. He is committed to making his vineyard—his wife and family—blossom. This is the biblical picture of being a husband.

Let me just stop at this point and reassure you that what she needs is clearly declared in Scripture. It is seven actions I'll take you through. You can do this. They will eventually become simple and easily done. I constantly say to husbands, "If I can learn them and do them, then anyone can learn them and do them."

## Knowing What Your Wife Really Needs

I have been teaching these marriage principles for decades now, and I have witnessed some dramatic results where they are practiced. Most husbands *want* to love their wives and are really *trying* to do so, but they do not know *how* to love her in a way that is meaningful to her.

When I ask husbands, "Do you love your wife?" most of them say, "Yes, of course!" This often comes with a look of incredulity from the wives, communicating, *Yeah, right. You'd never know it.*

Then I usually follow with this question, "How do you demonstrate your love to your wife?"

Practically every man I have ever counseled straightens up in his chair and proudly says, "I bring her my paycheck. I just bought her a new refrigerator. She has her own car; I got her that new dress last Valentine's Day..."

His wife will roll her eyes, a look of disgust registering loud and clear. Almost all the ways a man *naturally* loves his wife are material provisions. He often has no clue that she has relational needs that are going completely unmet.

I always respond the same way. "That's great. So, you show your wife you love her by providing for her needs and some of her wants. Let's talk about what love is. Love is meeting needs, pursuing, and pleasing. Let's say your wife has 100 needs in her life that you can meet. Let's say that she has ranked them according to how important they are to her."

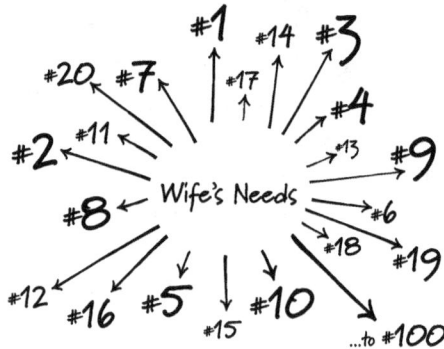

Continuing, I say, "Now, on your wife's list of her top 100 needs, let's say the ones you are meeting are number forty-six, sixty-seven, eighty-three, and ninety-seven on her priority scale. Let's say that the top twenty-one needs your wife has (the ones that are the most important to her—the ones discussed in this book) are not getting met. If I were to ask your wife, based on the needs you are currently meeting, 'Do you feel loved by your husband?' what do you think she would say?"

Finally, the light of understanding turns on in his mind, and he says, "Well, I suppose she would say that I don't love her all that much."

*Bingo!*

Then I give him a bit of hope by saying, "I am totally convinced you love your wife and want to love her, but you don't understand what her needs are. If I can explain the top twenty-one needs of your wife in a way you can understand and you begin to meet them, she will feel loved and excited about your marriage. These things do not come naturally for guys."

The great trouble destroying most marriages today is not meeting needs. The truth is that women have different needs than men, and he cannot figure out how to love his wife by thinking about what he needs or asking another man. The good news is that God has revealed in Scripture what a man must do to meet a woman's basic needs in marriage. I have found men can start meeting their wife's needs almost immediately but that it takes about three years before he really grasps the depth of her needs. But if he embraces his responsibility as the husband of the marriage and puts into practice the principles taught in Scripture, he will have a totally different marriage very soon.

Let me hasten to add that in many cases, these biblical principles run exactly counter to the way men have been taught to behave. God's principles tear at some of the most long-standing male attitudes toward women. Many men naturally move their marriages into a business relationship, which is seen today as an old-fashioned marriage. This is where the man has his interests and friends, while the woman has her interests and friends. They get together to discuss the house and kids, and for sex. This way of relating is perfectly satisfactory to many men, and they would sustain this kind of lifestyle indefinitely if they could. But this kind of marriage is not the kind of marriage Scripture teaches about. Women find this kind of marriage deeply unsatisfying and irritating. They want an intimate marriage—one with security, deep communication, and honor. They want an involved husband who invests his time and energies into the marriage and the children.

## Begin Today to Meet Her Needs

Whenever I reveal the list of actions that husbands need to do to properly love their wives, I usually get two different forms of pushback.

The first reaction is that this is impossible, or it would require him to give up his life to do all of these things. While this is not true (it only feels that way to the average man), I point out God's mandate that the husband should give himself up for his wife just as Christ did for the Church (Ephesians 5:25). Loving your wife in these ways does change your life, but in an enriching way that you can only barely comprehend at this point. As you begin to make these relational changes, oftentimes, your career opportunities improve, and most of the time, the relationship you have with your children will also improve dramatically. There is a great blessing in doing things God's way.

The second reaction I get is a comparison response, "What about Bill and his wife? He doesn't do any of this and she loves him incredibly." Husbands will often talk about some man they know who is a real jerk but whose wife still loves him. Then they wonder why their wife can't be more like this other man's wife! I usually let them know that they don't really understand all that is going on in that other man's marriage.

I have provided a list of seven affirmations to say each day until acting this way is second nature. They remind us of what we want to be like and serve as goals and rewards that compel us forward. Read this list every day for three months and watch as your marriage leaps forward in ways you can't imagine. Remember, it can take three full years for these principles to become second nature.

1. I HONOR my wife by making her my number one priority, next to God, by complimenting and praising her, eliminating disrespect towards her, and telling her I love her every day.

2. I UNDERSTAND my wife by knowing she is more sensitive than I am, by apologizing when I offend her, and by knowing her personality, family patterns, leadership styles, love languages, and past baggage.

3. I make my wife feel SECURE: financially, emotionally, physically, and spiritually.

4. I BUILD UNITY and direction in our family by engaging in lots of positive, shared experiences by never letting her be the enemy, describing the bright future we are headed towards, and being open to growing as a person.

5. I promote AGREEMENT between us by working through a wise decision-making process and forming and sticking with preset decisions. I don't insist on my own way, rather I pursue wisdom in coming to an agreement. She and I are a team.

6. I NURTURE my wife's full potential by engaging her in deep conversation every day, understanding and leading her spirit, pursuing her each week through dates, and tender, non-sexual touch.

7. I DEFEND my wife from all toxic spiritual, mental, emotional, relational, and financial threats, as well as physical threats.

## Where Is Your Wife on the Needs Continuum?

Every wife is different in their level of needs. Some women require lower levels of maintenance (requiring almost no maintenance, very independent), and some require higher levels (requiring a lot of maintenance, very dependent). You could really put various women on a continuum for how much of these loving actions they need from their husbands. All wives need and want these actions from their husbands in varying degrees—some need high levels of these actions to function and some not as much. Some husbands try to manipulate their wives to lower what she needs but this never works. She needs what she needs and will not blossom until she receives that amount.

Think for a moment about where your wife is on this continuum. Place a checkmark in the boxes below indicating where you feel her need level is for each action.

H U S B A N D

Highest

Medium
High

Medium

Medium
Low

Lowest

Key:

H - Honor
U - Understanding
S - Security
B - Building Unity
A - Agreement
N - Nurture
D - Defender

## Three Exceptions to the Plan Working

This plan has worked for many, many marriages that I know of, including my own marriage. But there are at least three exceptions where this plan is harder or won't work at all.

**A hardness of heart.** Jesus talked about this condition in Matthew 19:8. This is a condition of apathy or lack of caring about the relationship on either spouse's part.

**The abandonment of the marriage.** Scripture calls out a number of situations where the abandonment of the marriage manifests (Matthew 5:27–32; 1 Corinthians 7:10–16). Adultery, neglect, abandonment, and lack of forgiveness are a few of these.

**A deeply damaged past.** Proverbs 30:21–23 says, "Under three things the earth quakes; And under four it cannot bear up." One of these is "an unloved woman when she gets a husband." If a woman has never really been loved by anyone, she will often look for too much from her husband.

As you go through this book, take each chapter one at a time and figure out how to love your wife in this way. As you practice the exercises, I am confident you will see incredible changes. The ultimate goal is marital harmony and unity—the two of you working together to build a great marriage.

# PRINCIPLE #1—HONOR

---

"You husbands in the same way ... show her honor as a fellow heir of the grace of life, so that your prayers will not be hindered."

1 Peter 3:7 NASB

---

O ne **Monday evening,** I received a phone call from a man in my church. Jerry had just arrived home from work, and his wife and kids were gone. He didn't think much of it at the time, but when he came to the kitchen, he noticed a note on the refrigerator. It read, *"I can't live like this anymore! The kids and I left."*

Needless to say, he was completely shocked. He had no idea what to do and no clue where they went. He kept repeating, "My wife is gone, my wife is gone"—it was hard for him to get much else out. I tried to get the details, but he didn't have any. There had been hardly any arguments, and according to him, they were getting along just fine. From his point of view, there had been no problems; life was good. He had just come home that night, and she was gone.

I asked him to come over to talk, thinking I knew what was probably going on. I remember him holding the note as he walked up to my front door, shaking his head in disbelief. The first thing out of his mouth was, "How do I fix this? I didn't even know there was a problem!"

As we talked, I told him there were likely only two viable explanations for his wife's behavior: 1) either she was having an affair, or 2) he had not valued her as a top priority for so long that she felt used, worthless, and abandoned. He had trouble believing either one.

Since I knew them both well, I seriously doubted it was an affair, but I also knew she had a low self-image. He was a typical husband who went to work, coached baseball teams, went to the races, and usually stopped at home long enough to eat, sleep, and have sex. From his point of view, his marriage was a total success. But from his wife's perspective, it was a disaster. She needed him to value her, to want to talk to her. He always chose to spend his time, attention, and money on other things and other people. After fifteen years of living in a marriage like this, she finally broke down and left.

You see, Jerry had built a one-way marriage that worked perfectly for him, but he had given little to no thought about his wife's relational needs. He had given her his paycheck, but it hadn't occurred to him that his wife had needs that were largely unfulfilled. I was surprised by his wife's disappearance, but I was sure she felt she had to do something to get his attention. This was probably a shot across his bow, saying, "I have needs that can't be ignored!"

Jerry listened while I explained how he could learn to love her in new ways. I wanted him to be ready to act differently when his wife was ready to talk. I sketched out the concepts of *Becoming a Godly Husband* beginning with honor—which is choosing to place his wife as the number one priority in his life. This concept helped Jerry tremendously as he began to realize he had been taking his wife for granted. He had done what he had wanted while paying little attention to her. When she called, he would need to listen to what she had to say and acknowledge he had not been placing her as a top priority.

As suspected, she called a day or so later. He listened and apologized for the way he had taken her for granted. Once his wife saw he understood, she came back home. It wasn't very long before she was bragging about what a good husband Jerry was becoming. In just a few short weeks, they were on their way to a marriage that was deeply satisfying to both of them.

Many husbands are in danger of losing their wives but don't even realize it. Many women don't actually leave—they just become bitter or distant or spiteful. Pay attention to these cues. They are signals that something isn't right. What can you do? Learn what it means to honor your wife. There is a lot at stake when your wife's need for honor goes unmet.

## What Is Honor?

Treating your wife with honor is one of the most significant things you can do. Honor means adding value to her life and assigning great worth to her.

$$\longrightarrow \text{Honor} = \text{Value} + \text{Worth} \longleftarrow$$

For your wife, honor is not just a desire or idle interest of hers—it is as basic a need as food and shelter. Just as a man craves and needs respect, a woman craves and needs honor. No other quality, thing, or activity will ensure a good marriage like honoring your wife. This is the place to start because your wife knows that if she receives honor from you, you will meet her other needs also.

Your wife's need for honor is a search for proof of her own self-worth in real, tangible terms. There is so much in a woman's world that screams "Insignificance!" "Inadequate!" "Worthless!" She needs you, her husband, to validate her immense value and worth every day. She will be drawn to who can send her those messages. Your wife cannot handle playing second or third fiddle to your job, hobby, the kids, some racecar, or a football team. If she believes she has lost first place in your heart, you will lose. She doesn't always mean to make you lose, but she is not able to respond positively when you rob her of honor.

You may have already experienced what this looks like. Maybe she seems less interested in you. She begins to nitpick at little things, mutters under her breath, or slams doors. This might seem trivial, like "She'll get over it," but over time, she will fail to reach her full potential without honor. A lack of honor tears her down and limits her, which limits your marriage and, believe it or not, your success as a man.

Her need for honor is what draws her to you. It is like a vitamin she must have to be her complete self. A great husband supplies this fuel for his wife:

---

"You husbands in the same way … show her honor as a fellow heir of the grace of life, so that your prayers will not be hindered."

1 Peter 3:7 NASB

---

What I know about God is that He does not command any of us to do the things we would do instinctively. He directs us to do the things He knows are good for us, but we wouldn't naturally do on our own. Honoring our wives is not part of the typical manhood training for men. We have to be told that this is critical.

You communicate value through your actions, words, and attitudes toward her. Many men often have a difficult time understanding this type of self-worth because theirs comes from accomplishments, work, and material success. A man's self-worth is not usually relationship-based as a woman's often is. Women are different. It's not that a woman doesn't derive some self-worth from her accomplishments, but those are not usually the largest part of her self-esteem. She constructs her self-worth from the quality of her relationships. If her relationships are good, then she is good. But if she senses the key relationships in her life (you, children, work, friends) do not value her, she feels worthless and unfulfilled. As her husband, you can and should actively work to honor her while also training your children to honor her as their mother.

## How Can You Honor Your Wife?

In the next three chapters, we will look at three ways to demonstrate honor:

Chapter 1—Choose Her as Your #1 Priority

Chapter 2—Eliminate All Forms of Disrespect

Chapter 3—Use Praise to Build Her Up

# 1.

# CHOOSE HER AS YOUR #1 PRIORITY

Most men tend to see life as a series of conquests.** Think about it. Once you conquer or win something, you're on to the next challenge. This is how many men see their wives—a contest they have already won. Maybe you were attentive and interested when you were dating because she had not been won yet. However, did you notice when your attention, natural interests, and intense desires drifted to other areas about six months after the wedding? Your wife is very aware of this drift of focus away from her. If you continue to allow it, a rift in the relationship forms. If you don't make adjustments, the marriage you both dreamed about will begin to die.

Treating her like she is the most prized and valuable person in your life communicates *honor* to her. She checks her value levels every day. She judges how important she is to you by how you talk to her, your tone of voice, whether or not you notice what she is wearing, if you compliment her on what she has done, if you do nice things for her, if you are more excited about something else happening that day than being with her, and so on. All of these and a hundred other clues tell her how valuable she is to you that day.

Think of honor like a pill you must give her every day, or else she shrivels up. Most marriages that end in divorce actually die due to a lack of respect and honor between the husband and wife. Many people think it is because of a lack of sex or financial issues, but those issues are just symptoms of a deeper issue—lack of respect and honor.

Why do so many men fail to meet this vital need in their wives? Usually, it has to do with the hundreds of things demanding their attention. But if you are going to have a good marriage, you have to make sure your wife gets a significant amount of your attention every day. Only when you really focus on honoring your wife every day will you have the kind of marriage to satisfy your deepest needs.

The number one pushback I get from most husbands is that there is not enough time to do all this. *Yes, there is.* You can honor your wife every day and still be successful in business, hobbies, society, and other pursuits—it's a matter of prioritization. History is full of examples of men who had great marriages and great careers—great people like Winston Churchill, George H. W. Bush, Jimmy Carter, and Billy Graham, among others. Let me also suggest that God is the most impressed by your ability to love the people closest to you, not the career you build (Matthew 22:37–39; John 13:34–35).

Here is a helpful graphic to help explain the differences in priorities between what a husband may choose and what God wants them to choose. He wants you to set up your priority list in a very specific way so your life will go well. Take a minute to review these.

| Husband's Priorities | God's Priorities |
|---|---|
| 1. Self | 1. God |
| 2. Football | 2. Wife |
| 3. Job | 3. Children |
| 4. Cars | 4. Self |
| 5. Recreation | 5. Work |
| 6. Video Games | 6. Church |
| 7. Kids | 7. All other things, people, or activities |
| 8. Wife | |
| 9. Church | |

When you look at these two lists, are you surprised? God's priority order is very different than what we would naturally choose on our own because people are generally self-focused. God wants us to be others-focused. That's why we have to be taught His ways.

In terms of people in your life, God wants your wife to rank the highest in your priority after Him—way ahead of things, other activities, other people, or other ways to spend your time. Why? Because she is the basis for your greatest message. She tells the world what kind of man you are and whether Christ has made a difference in you—if you glorify Him or not. How you husband her says a lot about you.

## Growth Exercises—Rank Your Priorities

1.  Rank your priorities as they are today. What gets your most time, energy, attention, and money? Put what is most important to you in the first position (I am the most excited about this _____; I spend the most money on this _____ ; this always has my attention), and so on.

2.  Take time to pray and ask God to reveal how to adjust your priorities. What changes do you need to make regarding work, home, hobbies, activities, or friends?

3.  Some men have been willing to ask their wives what they think their husband's priority structure looks like. They actually know because they examine it every day. If you can handle the truth without getting angry, ask her.

**My Actual Priorities**

1.
2.
3.
4.
5.
6.
7.

## Passing Her Tests

Every day, your wife will run little tests to see how valuable she is to you. These tests are like little pop quizzes, like wanting to talk when watching a favorite TV show. She might ask you to take out the trash after settling into your chair. Maybe she'll call during your lunch hour to see if you want to talk. She may ask you to help her when you could be at the office or doing something else. All of these tests are designed to see you make a choice. It is in the choice that you reveal your priority, not what you say. She must see you choose her over something else; she can't just take your word for it. You need to pass them consistently for the effect to take hold.

I have been married for thirty-four years, and my wife knows that I love her and honor her, yet she still runs these tests every day. I realized a long time ago that my passing her tests is just another way to say "I love you" to her. Just tonight, she asked if I could take out the trash for her while I was in the middle of something else. I said,

"Of course I can, dear. I would be happy to." She heard, "I love you; I value you; I want your best." Passing the tests reassures her that you are paying attention and she is number one in your life.

Yes, it will take extra time and effort to register on her "he-values-me" scale. I have found that it takes between three months to one year of sacrificing and making sure you're putting her first every day before she really believes you mean it.

This concept is so important because she becomes a different person when her place of value is no longer threatened. She begins to reach for her potential. She'll encourage you to get back into your hobbies and friends. She is secure. Over time, the burden of honoring her will decrease and maintenance doses of honor are all that will be required. Most women believe their husbands will never pay the price of perpetual honor that wives so desperately need.

Some men honestly believe that honoring their wives at this level means the end of an enjoyable life as they know it. I remember one man lost all the color in his face when he grasped what I was saying about honoring his wife. He actually muttered, "My life is over." Reluctantly, he made the needed changes after I showed him in Scripture what God was saying. A month later, after passing lots of her tests, this couple was beaming about their new life together. His wife responded to his attention and honor in ways he did not expect. She blossomed, and he basked in the radiance of his new wife. He was paid back a hundred-fold for his investment in his marriage.

Think of this idea of honor as the oil in an engine. The engine doesn't run on oil, but it cannot continue to run without it. The oil level must be regularly checked because it lubricates all the friction needed for the engine to run and cools the heat that builds up. If you allow an engine to run on three quarts of oil when it needs four, it will still run, but as you know, it will wear out quicker and do damage as it runs. If you let an engine get all the way down to one or two quarts, it won't run for long. Displays of honor, value, priority, attention, and compliments are the lubricants for your marriage as they dissipate the heat that builds up by the two of you living together.

How do you know if she needs more honor? She may become irritable, critical, and tough to live with. These are all signals to you that she needs more honor. When there is enough self-worth flowing in and around your wife, the rough edges of the whole marriage smooth out, and the little difficulties don't even matter. Without it, everything is a big deal.

When I press husbands about passing these tests, they soon realize these are usually just a few minutes, not an endless list of chores. A little adjustment of your thinking will allow you to pass the tests and do what you want later. And many times, something better with your wife comes along.

## What Do You Value?

You set the value of the things in your life. If you decide something is valuable, it gets your time, attention, and money. I have seen men put a high value on comic books, video games, money, work, the garden, or their house. I even saw one man value a particular hedge in his front yard more than his wife and kids. I have watched too many businessmen consistently value their business over their wives and then wonder why she is so critical and negative. I recently heard a rich businessman get it when he told me, "I have worshiped money, and that is why my marriage is a total mess."

Unfortunately, many men let others convince them to put the wrong price tags or value on the things in their life. They value their jobs over their family, hobbies over marriage, and money over time with loved ones. The choices a person makes scream what they value. God says to value key relationships to build a successful life (1 Peter 3:7; Ephesians 5:25; Matthew 22:37–39). So when you put the correct amount of value and attention on the important people in your life, many good things begin to happen—your life becomes fulfilled. Many men are successful in terms of money, power, and influence but have very little of what they really want—love, joy, and peace of mind. Don't let this be you.

You selected this woman to be your wife. Choose to honor her every day by offering praise, value, love, and help. Choose to make your attitude, words, and actions say, "Today, I choose to honor you."

## Tangible Ways to Demonstrate Honor

Suppose a man chooses to value his wife and marriage. In that case, he will do the things that demonstrate it, like learning all about her, spending time learning how to make the marriage better, acting in new ways that bring honor to her, and spending some of his money on things that show her how much he values and appreciates her. All of these things will improve the relationship in drastic ways.

What are some ways you can honor your wife? Here are a few ideas that have worked for me and may work for you. Mark the ones you will try this week.

- Compliment her about something specific she did, said, or planned.
- Immediately turn off the TV or mute it when she starts talking to you.
- Get up right away and take care of your wife's issue.
- Practice manners—open doors for her, don't let her walk close to the road, help her into her seat.

- When you get home, ask her questions about her day and explore her thoughts.
- Follow her train of thought and conversation wherever it goes.
- Do something unexpected, like cook dinner, help with the dishes, vacuum, bathe the kids, offer to put the kids to bed, or give your wife the evening off.
- Ask her about her opinion of news stories or issues at work.
- Invite her to lunch sometime this week.
- Suggest an activity she finds enjoyable.
- Take the kids to the park to give her time alone if she needs it.
- Set time aside in the evening just to talk. Listen to her with intensity and focus.
- Ask her to go for a walk and be prepared with questions that draw out her thoughts.
- Set up a date every week to have fun and be together.
- Help her deal with a troubling or toxic relationship.

Most of these will take between five minutes to an hour but will pay rich dividends in your marriage. If you want a good marriage, you'll have to give up some time in your day to minister to your wife, and it will be worth it. Trust me.

# 2.

# ELIMINATE ALL FORMS OF DISRESPECT

I ran into Kevin and his girlfriend, Grace, at a weekend retreat. I had known them for about a year. They seemed like a lovely couple. He was a strong Christian; she a godly woman who was stunning in appearance. They got engaged and then married. I was shocked when I saw them at the retreat six months after the wedding—I could tell something was very wrong. Kevin was still very excited about the marriage, about his life, but Grace clearly looked exhausted and downcast. During the first few days of the retreat, I did not say anything. I just casually observed how Kevin was treating her. It was worse than I suspected. In an effort to be funny and the life of the party, he was constantly putting his new wife down. She was the butt of his jokes. She was always being corrected. Her comments were dismissed.

He had no idea of the verbal daggers he was thrusting into Grace's soul. With each passing day, she was under a thicker black cloud. The problem was clear. In what Kevin assumed was a good-natured way, he consistently tried to "help" her by pointing out areas where he thought she could improve. He joked about her weight. He laughed about her heritage. He ridiculed her personal habits. Everybody was laughing, but she was dying on the inside. He saw this as a double-win. He was popular in the eyes of the group, and she now knew what to work on to please him. This wasn't a big deal in his mind. He was only trying to motivate her to work on these areas—after all, it was done in jest.

After a few days of watching this, I pulled him aside and asked him if I could talk straight with him about his wife and his marriage. He had absolutely no idea that anything was wrong because few people ever corrected him. He said, "Sure, shoot straight." I told him I believed he had less than six months before his marriage would be over. He was emotionally destroying his wife, and she could not handle the daily barrage of his comments and digs. If he did not stop, she would be irreparably damaged, and he would be the loser. His wife was a treasure and a gift from God. Without even realizing it, he was changing this beautiful, intelligent, and vivacious woman into someone who would begin to repel him. The amazing thing was that he blamed her for becoming what he did not like. In actuality, he was the one at fault.

Kevin was stunned. No one had ever talked this straight with him. Everyone in his group said he was a great catch and a great husband. Fortunately, he listened to what I said. He set about digesting the information in this lesson and the entire *Becoming a Godly Husband* course. And most importantly, he eliminated the disrespectful comments and began to uphold her like the treasure she was. In a very short period of time, Kevin turned his marriage around. It didn't take long for Grace to start beaming about Kevin and her marriage. She had new motivation to become all God wanted her to be because her husband began honoring her.

It is very common for husbands to make their wives the brunt of jokes and humorous stories. This is tragic. Don't do it. Most men don't realize the high price they pay for their few moments of levity. Your wife needs honor. It is not something she can manufacture on her own. She is dependent upon the other people in her life to supply her with this substance she desperately needs. If she gets it, she will flourish and grow as a person. If she does not, she becomes unmotivated and often depressed. If you inject dishonor and disrespect into her life instead of honor, then the damage is more than double. She will be unable to grow, shine, or develop.

As her husband, you must do all you can to eliminate disrespect from her life. You do this by eliminating sarcasm and putdowns, backing up her weaker areas, and knowing where to inject honor and respect.

## Eliminate Sarcasm

Men can speak to other men in crude and sarcastic ways and think nothing of it. But this kind of behavior is toxic to a marriage. Women don't like it at all.

We live in a day when TV reinforces all the wrong images. Husbands get laughs when they send their wives a really good zinger, and the same is true for wives. But sarcasm is like pouring ice water down the front of your partner. It chills and abuses the relationship. It might seem fun at first, but the toxicity builds. Eliminate all sarcastic comments toward your wife even if she has gotten used to them or seems to like them and can give them back better than you. They do not ever help—they only make things worse.

Men always groan whenever I tell them that they need to eliminate sarcasm from their interactions with their wives. They pride themselves on how sarcastic they are. But from one sarcastic man to another, if you don't have anything to say without sarcasm, then say nothing at all. It would be better to say nothing if you do not have something helpful, loving, and constructive to say (Ephesians 4:29).

I spent much of my younger years developing a real gift of sarcasm and the funny put-down. I thought I was quite accomplished. But I found that this was a "skill" God wanted me to let die. I didn't realize that my sarcasm and put-downs were why all kinds of relationships in my life weren't working. I had dated many wonderful young ladies during my twenties, and every time I suggested we get serious, they would shy away and stop the relationship. Much of their fears centered around my sarcasm and lack of positive social skills. I was very funny in a group but devastating in one-on-one relationships. If I can learn to let go of sarcasm and be encouraging, anyone can. God had to show me how powerful positive words are and how damaging sarcastic words can be. It took me years before I didn't say every funny, sarcastic, or negative idea that came to my mind. I have a choice about what comes out of my mouth. I choose, with God's help, positive words.

I am amazed at how many men must learn a new way of talking and living with their wives when sarcasm is taken away. It is always a positive change. It can be a tough habit to break, but a little self-control is worth it. Sarcasm does not communicate clearly, and it destroys motivation for change.

If there is something she is doing that is threatening your marriage and must be changed, then sit down across from her, hold her hand, look her into her eyes, and say, "I have something very serious I need to discuss with you." Use soft tones and a loving context. If what you have to say is not significant enough to use this firm method, then let it go. I find this to be true for most issues.

## Back Up Her Weak Areas

Another way to show your wife honor is to focus on her strengths and not her weakness. She needs you to protect her weak areas, not expose them. As husband and wife, you are a team. Good teammates focus on their strengths, so their weaknesses become irrelevant. Your wife's job is to cover your weak areas, and your job is to cover hers. If she is not great with finances, don't have her do the finances! If she isn't an early riser, then allow her to do things later in the day. If she isn't the greatest housekeeper, find a way to help her—maybe do the work together, train the kids, or hire a housecleaner. If she isn't a great host for parties, don't insist on hosting parties at your house. Your job as a husband is to magnify her strengths, so her weak areas are not exposed to anyone. You are a team, and together you'll find solutions. She needs the energy your honor gives. When we truly value someone, we do not focus on their weaknesses but magnify their strengths instead.

It helps to develop a realistic picture of what your wife does well and what she will never do well. Then build your marriage where she does not have to expose her weakness. After my mom passed away, I asked my dad why we always had such unique birthdays. He told me that my mother didn't do parties well, so he decided to go to different museums, restaurants, and amusement parks for our birthdays so my mother's inability to throw parties would not be exposed.

---

"He who conceals a transgression seeks love,
but he who repeats a matter separates intimate friends."

Proverbs 17:9 NASB

---

Men, to a great extent, you can control what other people think about your wife. They don't live with her, and they usually rely on your comments to form their opinion. If you mention and highlight her positive qualities and strengths, their picture of your wife is positive and encouraging. Talking about another person's failures and mistakes is junior-high thinking. Everyone has weaknesses, failures, and foibles, but it is the job of those closest to them to protect them and leave people with a positive image of them.

I have helped repair marriages where the wife was a horrible cook, so the husband did most of the cooking. I have worked with marriages where the wife was not a tidy person, so the husband hired someone to come in and clean the house. I have worked with marriages where the wife was not interested in being creative in the sexual arena, so the husband provided the creativity and romantic elements for her to enjoy. I have watched great marriages where the wife was socially awkward, so the husband didn't put her in stressful social situations. I have helped marriages where the wife could not make her own friends, so the husband developed relationships with lots of people so his wife could have friends. I want you, as a husband, to imagine a marital life where your wife's weaknesses are minimized, and her strengths are on full display.

Another thing you can do is to guard your perception of your wife. If you keep talking about the negative stuff (what your wife does not understand, what she does not do well, how she messes up, inaccurate things she says), you will constantly be thinking about her weaknesses, and your attitude will sour towards her. But if you talk about her strengths with others (what she does well, what she really grasps with great ability, what she has mastered, what she is learning with great speed), your perception of her will increase. It is these seemingly little things that create a great marriage. I have been focusing on my wife's strengths for so long that I'm no longer aware of any weaknesses she has. They must be there, but I don't spend any time on them, and they have receded from my mind. She's perfect to me.

Spend some time thinking back to when you dated your wife. It was her strengths that you automatically kept in view that led you to marry her. Usually, this automatic focus on her strengths gives way to focused attention on her weaknesses during the first year of marriage. Realize that if she has a weakness, she will never be able to correct it if you keep harping on it. The way to overcome the weaknesses is to maximize the strengths until the weaknesses are irrelevant. In many cases, the strengths produce feelings of love, so get back to those.

## Where to Inject Honor

### Protection

As a husband, your job is to insulate your wife from negative words that could damage her. She needs to sense that you will protect and honor her. Some people will barge into her life and dishonor her. Think of yourself as a greenhouse surrounding a tender plant, protecting it from the ravages of wind, rain, sleet, and other forms of harsh weather. Some men leave the wife to fight her own battles, and I suppose many of them can. But that is not the way a godly husband behaves. He defends his wife's value. He protects her. Your wife needs to be comfortable and open in your presence, confident you will have her back.

### Speech and Names

All couples give each other nicknames. Some may be terms of endearment, but others can be mean-spirited or sarcastic. Give your wife titles and nicknames that communicate respect and honor. Do not put her down with the way you talk about her; build her up instead. It doesn't matter that you have been calling her a negative name for a long time. Let her know that you have been inspired to focus on her strengths, and that is why you have started calling her smart, beautiful, loving, genius, and so forth. Be careful of a derogatory tone. No matter how she speaks of you, it is your responsibility before God to speak respectfully to her and about her to others.

## Manners

Show her honor by gentlemanly manners. Manners exist in every culture and are a way of showing value and importance. Use all of the ones from your culture to display how valuable and significant she is. Here are a few from my culture—open the car door for her, let her walk under the umbrella or the protected canopy. Check on her at a party or social function with regularity. Ask her regularly if she needs your help with anything. Let her walk on the inside of the sidewalk. Show your wife she is valuable, and you are aware of her presence through manners.

## The Kids

Your children are one of the constant sources of disrespect in your wife's life that you can control. Tell and demonstrate to the children how to address your wife with respect. Have them practice these ways of addressing her over and over again until they do so automatically. They have not learned it until they are doing it daily. Do not allow your children, or any children, to call your wife by her first name alone. It is "Mom" or "Mother." They are not her equal. She is their mother. Or if they aren't your children, it is Mrs. or Ms. in front of her last name. This may seem old-fashioned, but it is still a proper title of respect and honor.[2]

## Clothing

It is amazing how much value a woman feels if she is wearing the right clothes in the right way. This area of honor includes letting her purchase clothes and accessories that boost her self-confidence. If possible, don't allow her to wear clothing or jewelry that makes her feel less valuable, even if she is willing to sacrifice in this area. You want to have as many messages as possible sending the same signals: *you are valuable.* Often, a wife will consistently make sacrifices for the good of the kids, the marriage, or the budget. This is commendable in the short run, but it can cause your wife to feel less valuable in the long run. I can remember a pastor who was criticized for his wife's nice clothes. He took me aside and let me know that he wanted his wife to feel good about her appearance. She was important, and he wanted to let everybody know he valued her.

## The House

Another key area where your wife calculates her value is from her house. This is generally not true for you, but many wives see their house as an extension of themselves. She needs you to strategize with her on how to make the house a place of honor. Your wife has a standard or an image of what her present house should look like. What could you add or take away from the house to tell her she is valuable: a new paint job, new or different furniture, an interior decorator's ideas, new or different appliances, a new carpet, an addition? Having a well-put-together house can inject huge amounts of self-worth and value into your wife.

Also, eliminate the elements of disrespect from the house. If the house is full of wrenches or newspapers, dirty clothes, or unfinished projects, you send a message. If you let the house drift below her standard, you will suck the energy out of your wife. Every woman is different in terms of what she feels a house should look like. When a woman says that an action disrespects her, believe her. It does not matter if the act or item seems trivial to you. If she is serious, then it should be changed.

### Gratitude

We can think of a woman's self-worth as a boat floating in a small, man-made lake. The water level is the level of honor, respect, and praise in her life. When the water in the lake goes down, the boat goes down. In this lake are submerged memories. When exposed, they destroy your wife's self-worth. They may be old relationships she had. They may be deep wounds from her childhood. They may be sinful choices she has made. When these memories are exposed or remembered, they pull your wife down into a cycle of depression, anger, and fear resulting in a lack of energy. Disrespect drains the lake, and her ship of self-worth runs aground against these submerged dangers.

If you keep a consistent and regular flow of gratitude and honor flowing into her life, she can float over these past events. Your gratitude compensates and lifts her above the problems of her past. In many cases, you, as her husband, are one of the critical sources of respect in her life. But you also can be a source of pollution into this little lake of her self-worth. The lake will be fouled and drained if you spew sarcasm and negativity. I am regularly amazed at how wives can ride above the storms of life if they receive enough honor and gratitude from their husbands. I am also surprised at how no number of workplace honors, salary, praise, or even good looks can make up for the acid of disrespect from a husband. Eliminate disrespect and add as much recognition, praise, and respect as possible.

## Growth Exercises—Evaluating Disrespect, Sarcasm, and Areas of Dishonor

1.  Memorize Proverbs 17:9.

    "He who conceals a transgression seeks love,
    But he who repeats a matter separates intimate friends."

2.  Answer these questions to the best of your ability and write them down:

    *   Are there any positive names or titles you can give
        your wife?

    *   What three things could you do around the house
        to eliminate dishonor for her?

    *   What three house projects could you finish that
        would make an immediate difference?

    *   Are you sarcastic? What could you say instead?

    *   Are there areas of weakness that you need to
        plan around, so they don't show?

    *   What are five strengths of your wife you can focus on?

# 3.

# USE PRAISE TO BUILD HER UP

---

**D**an and Sharon's marriage was a disaster. Dan was unaware of how bad it was until Sharon moved out and filed for divorce. She was not going to put up with the neglect, sarcasm, and disrespectful behavior any longer.

When Dan first came to see me, he asked if I could talk with his wife to see if she would stay married to him. He realized that if Sharon went through with the divorce, it would destroy him financially. It was obvious he was only concerned about the money. I explained that I was very willing to help them repair their marriage. But I told him the truth—all the years of being ignored and devalued had driven her to this point. "If you learn how to honor your wife and focus on her strengths, you can potentially win her back," I told him.

Initially, he was only interested in stopping the financial consequences of his actions rather than appreciating his wife's strengths. But through an amazing God-moment, he realized that he had not valued his wife for twenty years, and now he was going to pay for it.

In the midst of his depression and the growing doom of this court date, he began the process of learning how to pay positive, focused attention to his wife. He also eliminated the sarcastic comments about her weight, hair, and cooking, and, most importantly, he focused on her strengths. She was a remarkable, loving woman with significant leadership, organizational, and entrepreneurial skills. In refocusing on his wife and God, he realized what a fool he had been.

It was amazing to watch Sharon respond to his new attitude and actions. She became a softer and more positive person. He was now genuinely seeing her good points and praising them. He realized what a wonderful woman his wife was and told her. He said, "I can't live without her, forget the money." He appreciated her perspective on things and her intelligence in matters, and he developed a new enjoyment for her presence. Within a few short weeks, they were talking about reconciling. A month later, the lawsuit that would have divided their assets was torn up and forgotten. Praise is powerful, especially when accompanied by honor with a capital "H."

This man's wife had not changed at all. He did. All those weaknesses and faults that bothered him for years were still there but had faded into the background. God helped him by bringing into focus her positive qualities and strengths. And as he kept his attention riveted toward those good things, his love for her was renewed, and she blossomed. God worked in both of their lives because of Dan's focus on praise.

## Praise Is a Choice

All people thrive on praise and appreciation, your wife included. So often, we treat those closest to us with the least amount of respect. In truth, the people we love the most should receive the most affirmation. If we took care to praise our loved ones every time we are with them, it would make a huge difference in our relationships. We can always find some new thing to appreciate about them. Look at what Ephesians 4:29 (NASB) says: "Let no unwholesome word proceed from your mouth, but only such a word as is good for edification according to the need of the moment, so that it may give grace to those who hear."

Many times, men hold back praise because it seems unnatural to them. In our negative society, praise and appreciation seem out of place, but they are needed even more. A husband should be the first to praise and appreciate his wife. His praise and encouragement are powerful in adding to her self-worth.

Praise is a choice you can make to strengthen your wife. Never pass up an opportunity to notice the things she does well, and praise her for them. She needs all the energy she can get to accomplish things for the family, you, and herself. Your praise energizes her.

I can remember the change in one woman who had left her husband when he began complimenting her every day. At first, she did not want to believe what he was saying—she thought I was making her husband say nice things to her. But every day, he was finding things to compliment about her. After a few weeks of it, she could see he really did love her. After three months of it, she knew it to be true, and she moved back in. Everyone moves in the direction of the positive voices in their life. If you choose to consistently point out your wife's positives, you can lead her to a better version of herself and refresh her at the same time.

## Growth Exercises—Choose Praise

What are five things you can appreciate about your wife?
(Consider her qualities, behaviors, attitudes, new directions, and so forth.)

1. I love how hardworking she is.

2.

3.

4.

5.

## Withhold Criticism

Praise can also come in the form of refusing to speak an unkind word. There are many times when another person has made a mistake or done something awful, and the tendency is to point it out. You don't have to be the one pointing out the flaws of others. It is *high praise* if you ignore the mistakes your wife makes and just comfort her. If she messes up, just be silent about it until after the emotional impact of the moment is over. You can autopsy the situation later if one is needed.

My wife is practically perfect and very rarely does anything wrong. In fact, in all of our years of marriage, she has only been "wrong" a handful of times. I remember the second time she was actually wrong about something. I was ecstatic about this. I was finally going to get my chance to point out the mistake and correct her. As I started praying about the upcoming conversation, I distinctly remember the Lord prompting me to let it go and love her more. I wrestled with Him for several hours over this. I argued, "This is my chance to really let her have it. If I let this go, I'll have to wait another six years before she messes up again!" Finally, after much struggle, the Lord won and gave me the energy to let it go. He began prompting me with ways to love her more. Lots of things jumped into my mind, like getting her a gift for all the work she did around the house. When she got home, we gave her the gift and she beamed and apologized for what had happened. Praise is sometimes not saying the thing you could have said.

## Growth Exercises—Withhold Criticism

1. Memorize Proverbs 18:21.

   *"Death and life are in the power of the tongue,
   and those who love it will eat its fruit."*

2. Can you recall an incident that happened in your marriage when you could or should have kept quiet and just loved your wife?

3. What will you do next time your wife makes a mistake? What are ways you can love her more?

## Make Praise Specific

Many people attempt to praise but give just a general, generic appreciation. Praise is most impactful when you are specific. The more specific the praise is, the more help it is to the person who receives it. There are many ways to break praise down to specifics. For example, don't say something benign like, "You are a great wife." Instead say, "I am really impressed with how you faithfully _____ (fill in the blank). "You are a great woman, and I'm glad we're married." Instead of "I really love you," say, "When I see you care for the kids, listen to their memory work, and fix their meals, I fall in love all over again."

Brighten your wife's day by commenting on something very specific. Thank her for a particular meal. Compliment her on a specific outfit. Tell her how much a conversation with her meant Tell her about any good feelings toward her. She will brighten—it is like a superfood for her soul.

## Make Praise a Regular Habit

All people need to receive regular praise—daily, weekly, monthly. Each day is another opportunity to praise your wife. One famous marriage counselor said, "I try and do three things for my wife every day—tell her I love her, compliment her, and help her in some way." Too often, our wives have to go a long time between praises, but she needs to be praised once a day.

There are certain times during the day when praise seems to go deeper and mean more to her. It is your job as a husband to know when these times are for your wife. Some women like praise wrapped in words, some like little gifts, some like extra help, and so forth. Find a way your appreciation will not escape your wife's notice.[3]

The only way she will know you notice what she does is if you tell her. This is what it means to love her. *She will also notice who gets the most praise in your life.* Many men praise their favorite sports team more than their wives. If you want to let her know that she is still number one, make sure she receives more praises than anyone else.

If you are putting your wife in the number one slot (right below God), she will naturally occupy more of your thoughts. Here's how it looks. You notice when she does certain things you like and make a positive comment about it. You notice when she looks beautiful to you and make a positive comment about it. You notice when she goes out of her way to please you and make a positive comment about it. You notice when she is sacrificing for the family and make a positive comment about it. You get the idea.

A prominent speaker years ago described how his marriage was not going in the right direction at one point in his career. It wasn't bad, but it wasn't great. He began to look at how he was treating his business clients and even the waiters at the restaurants. He noticed that he had been giving other people a better version of himself than his wife. His wife received the crabby, drained person who came home, dragging himself in at the end of the day. He told God and himself that he would never let anyone get better treatment than his wife ever again. This changed his marriage dramatically. When he noticed he was treating someone else really well, he would do the same for his wife. His wife began to see that she was equal to or more valued than every other person in his world and her response to him became so much better. Their marriage went from pretty good to great.

## Growth Exercises—Give the Best Version of Yourself to Your Wife

1.  Who in your life gets especially good treatment from you?

    | | |
    |---|---|
    | business associates | relatives |
    | friends | clients |
    | strangers | neighbors |
    | waiters | mail delivery |
    | police officers | workmen |
    | guests | pet |

2.  How can you translate this type of treatment to your wife?

## Three Types of Praise

### Verbal Praise

Verbal praise is the most difficult and threatening type of praise because it usually involves telling your wife something good about her face-to-face. You can develop helpful phrases that make the process of verbal praise easier. Some examples might be:

"I am so proud of you when you ..."

"I can't even tell you how good it makes me feel when you ..."

"I noticed the other day when you ... and I just wanted to say thanks."

"You are something special. I saw when you ..."

### Written Praise

This type of praise involves praising your wife in some written form. It can be long or short. It can be fancy or informal. It can be a story, a poem, or just a line in a text. There are an endless number of ways to write what is praiseworthy about her.

### Tangible Praise

This type of praise involves giving your wife something tangible to say that you think she is doing a great job. This could be the unexpected box of chocolates, flowers, or any special gift. This is anything she can touch that says, "I'm thinking about you, and you're doing a great job."

Remember, each woman is different. Your wife may embrace your praise better if it is verbal rather than written. She may get more energy from tangible praise than from verbal praise. She may take the greatest delight in re-reading your notes of appreciation and encouragement. She may enjoy trophies or gifts that remind her how valuable she is to you. These are like permanent markers she has all over her life that you value her. How many does she have now?

Study your wife for what she responds to the best. It is a husband's job to add value to his wife so she has the energy to glorify God maximally. Test each of these ways of complimenting your wife for maximum impact. Use the best ones over and over again.

## Growth Exercises—Practice Praising Her

What is one verbal, written, and tangible praise or gesture you could make to your wife this week? When and how will you do these?

1. Text her about how much I appreciate her.

2.

3.

## Three Forms of Praise

### Direct Praise

The direct form of praise—verbal, written, or tangible—happens when you are the person that presents the praise, and your wife is the one who receives it. There is an immediate interaction between you and her in this form of praise.

Your wife may like when you send her a text about something really positive or something she may not have realized was praise-worthy. She may like these direct, "I-think-you-did-great" comments.

### Indirect Praise

This form of praise—verbal, written, or tangible—occurs when you are not present when your wife receives the praise. This means someone or something gives her the words of encouragement on your behalf.

Some women light up when they hear their husbands praise them to a co-worker or one of their girlfriends. This is such a powerful delayed way of uplifting people.

### Symbolic Praise

This form of praise—verbal, written, or tangible—happens when your praise is put in symbolic forms. This could be a symbol that everybody understands (a heart, diamond, or rose) or symbols that only you and your wife understand (letters or finger codes, made-up words, a visual symbol, and so forth). This may sound silly or needless, but special codes, names, signs, or symbols say your love is alive to your wife. I remember one woman who loved elephants, so her husband bought her an elephant on every business trip he went on. This said to her that he was thinking of her while he was gone. One woman I knew loved salt and pepper shakers, so her husband made sure they went into all kinds of curio shops and bought another salt and pepper shaker to commemorate every trip they went on.

## Growth Exercises—How Will You Praise Her?

What is one direct, indirect, and symbolic praise or gesture you could make to your wife this week? When and how will you do this?

1. Bring her a coffee to work on Tuesday.

2.

3.

# PRINCIPLE #2—UNDERSTANDING

"You husbands in the same way ... show her honor as a fellow heir of the grace of life, so that your prayers will not be hindered."

1 Peter 3:7 NASB

❦

Your wife is perfectly and uniquely made for you. Do you believe that? God has given her all sorts of gifts, talents, and abilities, a unique temperament that helps her process her thoughts and emotions, and a way of making decisions that makes sense to her. She also has many hidden factors in her thought processes that you do not have or do not utilize. The problem is that many husbands don't take the time to figure out all those unique and interesting factors that make up her being. They falsely believe their wives are illogical, a puzzle that can't be solved. You can imagine this type of thinking leads to a lot of frustration and misunderstandings in the marriage.

I think you will find that your wife is not illogical but perfectly logical if you can begin to understand all the factors she brings to bear in life. She weighs relational factors plus her unique temperament, abilities, feelings, and experiences to help her arrive at her decisions. She can often accurately predict three or four levels of the way people will react to specific actions and statements. For example, "If we do this, then my brother will do that, and then you will feel the need to say this, and it will result in a horrible Christmas." She is an incredible person you need to know.

Let me tell you the tragic story of one man's failure to understand the people in his life. Several years ago, famous movie director and actor Woody Allen was getting a divorce from his wife. He was suing for joint custody of his children. He told the judge that he loved the children and wanted to remain involved in their life. The judge listened to his declarations of love for his children; then, he began to test Mr. Allen to see if his words were true. The judge asked Woody Allen, "What is your son's favorite toy?" "What is his favorite color?" "Who are his closest friends?" "What is his favorite book?" "What is his routine on a weekday?" "What are your son's concerns in this divorce?" "What does your son want to be when he grows up?"

Each of these questions from the judge received a blank stare and then an "I don't know" from Mr. Allen. Finally, the judge ruled, "Mr. Allen, a parent who really loves his children, understands what is going on in their lives and knows the details of their lives and their dreams. I suspect, Mr. Allen, that you don't love your children nearly as much as you want me to believe because you know none of these things."

I have been around a lot of couples in great marriages. I love asking people questions who have been in long-term relationships and are still in love. One element that stands out in great marriages is that couples know each other from a positive point of view. They can finish each other's sentences. They know the other's preferences. They know each other's likes and dislikes. This concept of understanding seems to come more naturally to the wife. But what separates the great marriages from the bad ones and run-of-the-mill marriages is when the husband knows all about his wife too. He studies her and embraces her differences in a positive way. Enjoy getting to know and understand your wife in a deeper way.

## What Does It Mean to Live with Your Wife in an Understanding Way?

In the following three chapters, we will look at three subcategories of what you can understand about your wife:

Chapter 4—Her Sensitive Nature

Chapter 5—Her Personality

Chapter 6—Her Need to See You Improve and Become Wise Over Time

# 4.

## HER SENSITIVE NATURE

"You're too emotional!"

"You're too sensitive!"

"Stop crying!"

**With these and other cutting remarks,** Carl demonstrated over the years that he really didn't understand his wife, Ashley. His gruff treatment and total insensitivity were slowly destroying her. At one point, Ashley laid down in the hallway after another one of his thoughtless remarks to illustrate how his comment had just wiped her out. She had left him on more than one occasion to try to get him to understand that she and the children could not put up with this kind of treatment.

Ashley lived on this roller coaster for over ten years until she fled from him to save her emotional wellbeing. He never stopped believing that if his wife would just toughen up and be a good wife, their marriage would be fine. Last I heard, Carl was working on his second marriage.

Another couple I have visited many times, John and Elizabeth, also struggled from a failure to understand how a woman typically responds to certain situations. On one occasion, John stood over his wife, with his six-foot-three-inch frame, yelling down at her, "I am not threatening you! I would never hurt you!"

Elizabeth was petrified with fear over his behavior and bad temper. He was absolutely destroying her. She was a strong woman but also sensitive. She was trying to live with this man she loved while being emotionally traumatized by his anger. It is the husband's job to create harmony in the home. Your anger won't accomplish this.

Elizabeth left home on several occasions, sometimes for up to a week, to calm the situation. Finally, John began to see that the way he was trying to fix the problems was not working. He began trying to understand his wife. His wife responded positively to his newfound tenderness. She deserves great praise for being willing to persevere while he learned to treat a woman in an understanding way.

## The Buffalo and the Butterfly

Buffaloes and butterflies. Rocks and pebbles. I like to use this analogy first given to me by best-selling author Gary Smalley to help men understand a woman's sensitivity and how different it is from a man. Most men are like buffaloes, with thick skin that doesn't feel the slights and offenses of others. Men can treat each other with callous disregard and then still be friends, thinking nothing of the comments, name-calling, and lack of attention. Men tend to believe their wives ought to be able to take the same type of punishment their workmates or friends receive. He'll usually defend his insensitive words or actions with comments like, "I didn't mean it!" "It was only a joke!" "C'mon, you're overreacting!" "I do this with everyone."

God created men and women with varying sensitivity levels for good reasons. Neither one is better than the other; they are just different. Many husbands accuse their wives of being overly sensitive. In many cases, your wife has sensitivities to things you don't sense at all. Where is she on the various sensitivity scales? Her level of sensitivity can be a huge positive in the marriage and not a hindrance. Think about it. The most valuable electronic gear is the most sensitive. The most high-priced speakers are the most sensitive to different pitches, tones, and volumes.

In most cases, your wife was not built to be rugged; she was designed to be sensitive to enhance life and help you grow. God made women more like butterflies—beautiful creatures with delicate wings borne along with the slightest breeze. They are fragile and easily broken if you don't handle them with care.

If you liken your words to pebbles and stones, you'll begin to see my point. Let's say you throw a pebble at the buffalo. It is hardly felt at all—a minor annoyance, a tap. But if you take the same pebble and throw it at a butterfly, it would devastate this little creature. In the same way, offenses that make no impact on many men (or are hardly felt at all) devastate our wives and cause them great pain. What may only be a pebble to us buffaloes is a giant boulder to our butterflies. The same insult that works as a joke at work is a huge boulder crushing your wife. Your wife is not too sensitive; she is exactly how God made her.

Some women diagnosed (often by men) as "emotionally unstable" are trying to dodge boulders being thrown at them. It is up to you, her husband, to understand how sensitive your wife is. Yes, some women are more sensitive than other women. A super-sensitive wife is a great thing, just like a super-sensitive microphone or metal detector. If your wife is especially sensitive, how you treat her will need to be adjusted. I talk to men all the time about ratcheting up their behavior to fit in with their wife's sensitivity. If they do, it almost always translates to promotions, friends, job offers, and a much better marriage. If you want your marriage to be great, then talk, act, and provide an environment your wife can thrive. Yes, men, you can do this. If you can learn to thrive with your wife's more delicate emotions and sensitivities, then your children can grow up free from your anger and achieve their full potential too. Isn't that what you want?

## How Your Wife Thinks and Makes Decisions

Your wife is not illogical or too emotional, or too sensitive. She merely thinks differently than the typical man. Most men don't believe it's possible to understand how their wives think and how they arrive at their decisions. This is a male myth. God says women are understandable. Thinking involves a series of choices. If we knew what other people were thinking, we could understand the choices they make. Most women consider feelings as mental change points, which most men do not. ("I wouldn't want to say that because my mother would feel terrible.") Most women consider reactions and attitudes as potential change points, which most men do not. ("I couldn't do that because my friend would consider that a betrayal, and I can't lose that friendship.") Men tend to think of feelings and reactions as the fog that needs to be pushed through. These emotional elements are not real enough for most men to change one's minds or do something different. Your wife is perfectly logical if you factor in emotions and reactions as real elements.

Think of a pinball game where the middle of the game is blocked from your view with a sheet of paper. If there were no gears or levers behind the paper, the ball would enter the top of the game and fall to the bottom in a predictable line. This is how many men see decisions being made. This, to them, is logical. They present the facts as they see them and then expect the same conclusions they have made. They are shocked when their wife reaches a totally different conclusion. Why does she do this? Because she is considering reactions, feelings, attitudes, and experiences that he has never considered. The paper covering the middle

of the pinball game hides all kinds of bumpers, paddles, holes, and ramps that send the ball (decisions) in entirely different directions. Your wife is completely logical in her thinking if you recognize these extra parts of her mental processes as real. Remember, she is more sensitive to these realities. Yes, some of her mental and emotional redirects may be mistaken, just as some of yours are, but she is perfectly logical about why she makes the decisions she does.

## She Has Gifts That You Don't

Your wife is an amazing creation whose sensitivity level is most likely beyond yours. Did you know she visualizes or pictures scenarios totally different than you? Let me give you an example of what I mean. If you are going out, she will ask, "Where are you going?" You will say "Target." In your mind, as a guy, you will see the Target sign and the front of the store. But almost every woman who has been to a local Target will see a three-dimensional rendering of her local Target with the roof pulled off. She will then ask you, "What are you going to get?" If you tell her, she will go there in her mind with you and she'll even know the other parts of the store you'll be walking by. Naturally, you'd be able to "grab" a few things for her on your way through the store. It's as if she is right there with you in her mind if given enough details.

This also means she is able to experience trips you take in her mind if you give her enough of the details. She really does want to be with you and has the ability to do it if you walk her through the specifics. When I have returned from business trips in the past, my wife would often say, "How did it go?" I used to say, "Fine." But I realized that she couldn't be on that trip with me if I just say "fine." I needed to let her know what the hotel was like. What the conference was like. How people responded to my speech. Who I went to dinner with. Where I went to dinner and the foods I ate. The more details I gave her, the more she could paint a picture in her mind that she could live in with me. Many husbands ask why they should go to all of this detail. It's simple. Doing so allows you to build a great relationship with your wife, which is the whole goal, isn't it?

In addition, since your wife is able to see the world from a more relational position, she needs to know the "who" before she can discuss the "what." She is far more sensitive to interconnections between people and offenses that can take place between people than you will most likely ever be. Her heightened sensitivity can be very helpful in many situations.

Let me state it plainly:

*Your wife is more sensitive than you, but she is not too sensitive.*

*Your wife is more easily wounded than you are, so you need to apologize more frequently.*

*Your wife is able to visualize what you say and it becomes real to her, which you don't do.*

*Your wife has desires, abilities, and impulses you don't have, which will deeply enrich your life if you understand and embrace them.*

*Your wife is in touch with her emotions, others' reactions, and attitudes that you are not.*

*Your wife's thinking process is more involved than yours because she includes emotions, reactions, and relationships that you don't.*

## Growth Exercises—Where Is She on the Sensitivity Scale

1.  Memorize 1 Peter 3:7a.

    > *"You husbands in the same way,*
    > *live with your wives in an understanding way,"*

2.  Rate your wife's sensitivity level on a scale of 1 to 10, taking into consideration how she responds to put-downs, anger, insensitivities, with 10 being the most fragile, and 1 being not sensitive at all.

    1    2    3    4    5    6    7    8    9    10

3.  In what areas is she the most sensitive? Study the areas where you believe her reactions to some of the things you do or say are fragile or emotional. List them below.

4.  Make a list as long as you can describing the benefits of your wife being as sensitive as she is.

## Know When She Is Hurt

When people really hurt us, either by stepping on our feelings, damaging our integrity, taking advantage of our vulnerabilities, or causing us physical pain, we close up to them. Just like how a flower closes up at night, we do the same thing to those who wound us. Our personality is not as bubbly and encouraging. We engage that person less. We have less to talk about. We take a defensive posture towards them. This is especially true if the wounds have been repeated and the person does not show any signs of letting up. Eventually, we can become so closed that we can barely even speak to them, let alone be around them. This happens in marriages all the time. It is one of the primary reasons women divorce men. They get hurt so often that they shut down towards their husband. If your wife is closed towards you or unwilling to let her touch you, then they have been wounded by you.

All people are made up of three parts. Those three parts are like concentric circles, one inside another. First, we have our spirit (the place of creativity, conscience, security, significance, personality); second, our soul (mind, will, emotions, where conversational ability comes from); and third, our body (physical touch, intimacy, deep feelings, and sexual relations).

(least open)   1
2
3
4
5
6
7
8
9
(most open)   10

BODY

SOUL

SPIRIT

You can tell which part of her is hurting by how she acts and relates with you. Depending on which of her three parts is hurting tells you the level and depth of her woundedness. For example, if you are the person who has hurt her, you may observe she no longer shares her new ideas with you or the outgoing parts of her personality. Nine times out of ten, this is because you have hurt her, and her *spirit* is closing up. If she no longer talks with you about what she thinks, feels, or wants to do, she is even more closed towards you—her *soul* is closing up. If she moves to another room when you enter the room, refuses your touch, or almost always rebuffs sexual relations. In that case, you can be absolutely sure you have hurt her deeply, as her very *body* is significantly closed to you.

As husbands, we don't intentionally set out to hurt our wives, but sometimes we do. We must be ready to fix this situation.

## Growth Exercises—Testing for Openness

1. When your wife is open to you, how does she act toward you? What about when she is closed? What have you noticed?

2. On a scale of 1 to 10, with 10 being completely closed (she cannot stand to be in your presence) and 1 being completely open (holding nothing back from you), rate your wife's response.

1   2   3   4   5   6   7   8   9   10

## Steps to Recover Openness

What do you do if you have hurt her? I see couples where the husband has wounded his wife but doesn't know how to get his wife back to a place of openness. As the husbandman, it is your responsibility to take the necessary steps toward harmony. The gardener wants to make sure that the vineyard blossoms and grows. If you have wounded or offended her, you need to know how to repair the damage.

I can remember when my mentor shared these golden steps for how to repair a relationship when you have damaged it. It was like I was given the secret key to a woman's heart! I memorized these steps. I used them to repair all kinds of relationships. The more I practiced them, the better I got at using them. I blew up fewer relationships. You and I will offend and wound the people we love and work with; it's part of being human. But there are secrets we can employ to repair those relationships. Treat this material wisely because it really works.

*Step One—Approach her with a gentle spirit.*

Be soft and gentle in your tone of voice and spirit whenever a problem or offense has been made. You need to understand whether or not you are the one who caused the problem. You have to come softly and humbly to your wife, or she will not tell you what is going on. If she does not respond, be even more soft and gentle. Many wives change their whole demeanor when their husbands are finally soft and gentle enough. It is very difficult to stay upset at a person who is gentle, calm, and quiet, as this Scripture teaches,

"A soft answer turns away wrath, but a harsh word stirs up anger."
Proverbs 15:1 RSV

———

*Step Two—Ask her to educate you.*

When we offend our wives, we don't know what we did wrong most of the time. Also, we often do not know the whole of the offense. We also don't know what it felt like from her perspective. Ask your wife to educate you. Assume that you are the cause of the problem. Let her tell you if you are *not* the problem. The Bible calls this kind of openness *seeking a rebuke*. It is based on what is taught in Luke.

"If your brother or sister sins against you, rebuke them;
and if they repent, forgive them."

Luke 17:3 NIV

———

If you ask your wife what is truly wrong and stay gentle, she will tell you. She might only tell you part of the problem initially to see if you are willing to listen. Stay soft and keep seeking to understand the full nature of the problem.

At first, there are times when she does not know why she is feeling wounded. It may take a while before she can pinpoint what wounded her. Keep asking questions in a calm manner. The fact that you want to understand is a huge fix for the problem.

Most husbands who seek to understand the problem will eventually hear the real problem. I can remember one time when I was dating my wife, I hurt her, and it took around forty-five minutes of listening and asking questions to get to the real issue.

You need to understand the significance of the offense. She cannot just "get over it." She needs you to understand what causes her to break down. Remember, she is not you, and it doesn't matter if you wouldn't be wounded by what you did or said. She was. You want a relationship with her, not with yourself.

### Step Three—Confess your offense.

Once you know what the offense is and that you were the cause of the offense, then you can simply and humbly say, "I was wrong when I _____." It is not usually enough to just say, "I'm sorry." Your wife wants to know that you realize what you did wrong. If you confess the wrong thing, you prove you were not listening carefully or are not truly sorry.

A sincere, deeply felt, "I was wrong when I disrespected you by not calling to tell you that I would be late" will go a long way in repairing the marriage. "I was wrong to forget our anniversary." "I was wrong when I insulted your mother." When men understand how their comments or lack of action can deeply wound their wives, then they will be able to apologize sincerely.

### Step Four— Ask for forgiveness.

When you have admitted that you did something wrong, you can ask for forgiveness. I usually find it helpful to say something like this: "I know I don't have any right to ask you to forgive me, but would you forgive me?" Then wait for the yes or the no. It is important to have her verbally forgive you.

If she will not say she forgives you, go back to the beginning and become more gentle in your approach, seeking more education about what offended her. There may be more to the offense that she has failed to share up to this point. I know this sounds like a very involved process, but this kind of clearing the air and getting past hurts is essential for a growing marriage. Remember, your offenses are like boulders on her wings. She can't fly if there are still boulders crushing her. This process usually takes between forty-five minutes to ninety minutes to complete. It is never fun, but a great marriage is worth this work.

This whole process aims for you to learn what caused damage to her so you won't do it again. Many men will admit they were wrong to get past the tension, but they don't plan on changing. She wants to know that you will do everything possible not to hurt her again. There can't be just a surface apology.

*Step 5—Repent with a plan.*

For some deep offenses, you will need to suggest a repentance plan. What most wives are looking for is a plan that *demonstrates in real life* that we are serious about changing. I find that too many couples do not have a way to help improve in needed areas, so the hurts just pile up until someone is so fed up they move toward divorce. Don't let this happen to you.

Too many women say, "My husband tells me he was wrong, but he keeps doing it." When you don't know how to solve the problem (as in the case of a recurrent one), ask your wife to help. She would love to help develop a plan that would demonstrate that you're serious about change.

There is a very real sense that you have not truly repented unless your actions prove it. Many people are tired of half-hearted apologies— "I'm sorry; won't you please let me slide this time?" This is not repentance; it is a hollow apology. If you have wounded another person, you must make sure you don't do that again. A repentance plan for serious or repetitive offenses will help with this. Below are a few examples of repentance plans for these possible scenarios:

| SCENARIO | PLAN |
|---|---|
| Repetitive Drunkenness → | Go to AA meetings regularly and respond to my text or call within fifteen minutes. |
| Failure to call from work if you were going to be late → | No dinner when you get home and take your wife out to dinner the next night. |
| Failure to pick up clothes → | Any loose clothes left on your side of the bed will not be washed until they are properly sorted, put away, put in the hamper, or otherwise washed by you. |
| Failure to clean up the kitchen after making a mess → | Must do all the dishes for the next day to remind you to clean up after yourself. |

*Step Six—Test for openness.*

If the above steps succeed, your wife will be open to you again. She will begin to show her personality and express her thoughts and feelings. And most importantly, she will allow you to reach out and touch her. If your wife still pulls away from you when you try to touch her, then she is saying she is not ready to forgive you. Go back to the beginning with a gentler spirit.

# 5.

## UNDERSTAND HER PERSONALITY

A woman came to see me in my office and blasted her husband with this statement, "I won't divorce him… but I will be gone—a lot. It is totally dissatisfying for me to be around that man." I probed a little deeper and discovered a very frustrated and discouraged wife. He didn't understand her, and she was losing it. He had not thought through what made his wife tick—her gifts, abilities, skill sets, temperament, motivations, love languages, or desires. He was being robbed of the wonders of her personality, and she was becoming increasingly caustic with him.

As I worked with this woman to discover who she was and how her gifts, abilities, and temperament could be used to benefit her marriage, she grew more and more excited about her marriage. Within two weeks, she had abandoned plans to divorce her husband emotionally. The lesson is this: *Don't underestimate the need for your wife to be understood and released in the direction of her gifts, talents, temperament, and desires.*

Another woman came to see me with a similar problem. She was also frustrated in her marriage and with life. After talking with her for a while, she was obviously trying to be someone she was not. When I described to her how she could express who she was, it didn't take long for her to brighten and enjoy life. She had unique leadership gifts that needed to be expressed and utilized. When it became okay to be who she was, the depression lifted.

A person's temperament is an internal mechanism that causes them to act in a certain way. It is often imperceptible to the people themselves, but they are consistently influenced in a specific direction. Some people seem to need to clean, some to speak their mind, some to be in charge, some to listen to the troubles of another, some to make peace, some to make decisions, and so forth. These internal impulses control the way we see life and act in the world around us. It is a husband's job to understand these factors in his wife and create a climate where she can pursue who God made her to be (Ephesians 5:25–28).

Remember, the great prize for understanding your wife is a great marriage. Your wife needs to be fully unfurled so that her strong points can shine. As the husband, you have the opportunity to help her live a much more impactful life. Think of it this way…if you were the head of a company and knew that the people on your team had undeveloped abilities, skills, and gifts, wouldn't you be excited about developing them? What hidden talents, gifts, or interests does your wife have that you might help develop?

## Understand Her Natural Abilities and Skills

Understanding your wife includes knowing her natural abilities and skills. Abilities are natural talents. Skills are routines and tasks she has learned to do. She is very good at some things and not good at others. Some women are great at things their husband is not. This can be problematic as each spouse tries to understand why the other person doesn't enjoy what gives them such pleasure. What skills does she have? Which ones would she like to develop? A basic way to tell if someone possesses a particular natural ability or skill is the ease they have when doing certain activities and the level of joy they feel.

It is very important to realize that just because you find an activity enjoyable, pleasing, or easy does not mean your wife will feel the same way. She may not have any natural inclination or ability in an area, which may be why she has avoided it.

Some levels of your wife's satisfaction and happiness are dependent upon being able to use and express her abilities, gifts, and skills. If she can't, for whatever reason, there will be a level of discouragement or anger. You can help her figure out what she enjoys with this simple exercise below. I have seen many wives who have growing boredom or anxiety with their life as the kids grow up and leave the house. If she doesn't find a way to use more of her abilities, dreams, and gifts, she could get discouraged as the picture of her future is vague. Help your wife discover how to make life an increasingly expanding adventure.

# Growth Exercises—Identify Natural Abilities and Talents

In the chart below, put an "H" by the top five activities that are true for you and a "W" by those that are true for your wife. Then observe and write down what you notice. Think about which ones you and your wife have been able to express in your lives lately and which ones are not being expressed. How can each of you express the things you are naturally good at?

| | | |
|---|---|---|
| Writing | Building | Counseling |
| Dancing | Performing/Acting | Analyzing |
| Leading | Singing | Teaching |
| Athletics | Music/playing an instrument | Coaching |
| Business | Cooking | Photography |
| Finances | Painting | Designing/Decorating |
| Reading | Directing | Coordinating |
| Persuasion | Medicine | Creativity |
| Selling | Gardening | Detail work |
| Hosting | Computing | Visionary |
| Organizing | Shepherding | Recruiting |
| Physical health & exercise | Other: | Other: |

## Understand Her Spiritual Gifts

Spiritual gifts are special abilities that God gives Christians. Do you know what your wife's spiritual giftings are and how often she gets to use them? One pastor I know states that the best way to live an amazing life is to find out what are your spiritual gifts and build your whole life around them. Find out what yours are and help her find hers.

There are over twenty different spiritual gifts that a Christian can receive (1 Corinthians 12:7). Each gift is a way that God's power flows through us to serve other people for the kingdom of God. For example, if your wife has the gift of prophecy, it usually means that she is not afraid to speak out when she sees something wrong. A mercy giftedness would demonstrate itself in your wife taking on the hurts and pains of other people. A teaching gift wants to explain concepts to others so they will grow in the knowledge of Christ. An exhortation gift wants to share practical steps of action and encouragement to mature as a Christian. A leadership gift wants to cast a vision for a better future and recruit people to accomplish that vision. A giving gift makes you aware of resources for God's projects.

Realize that each one of these gifts will influence your wife to act, react, and live differently. Her spiritual gifts are God-given impulses to act in a certain way. They will often determine how she perceives a problem or situation and her interaction with it.

All spiritual gifts are great blessings from God, but if you don't understand what the gift does and how it motivates or limits your wife, there could be a great deal of misunderstanding in the marriage. Talk with your wife to understand her gift mix and how best to use it.

### Growth Exercises—Determine Spiritual Gifts

1.  Determine your wife's top four major spiritual gifts. For a free spiritual gift assessment, go to **ptlb.com/discover-your-spiritual-gifts**. Both of you can take it, then share the results with each other.

2.  Think through and talk about what each gift does and how it motivates or limits you and your wife. How will each of you use the gifts God has given you to serve and edify His body?

## Understand Her Desires, Dreams, and Goals

Part of living with your wife in an understanding way is to explore her desires, dreams, and goals. Scripture suggests that husbands are the gardeners of their wives, so your success is determined by how your wife blossoms. You can be a huge success in business and still fail because your wife and family are dying from a lack of emotional, mental, and spiritual nutrients.

What does she want to see in the next five years regarding:

- her relationship with God?
- her marriage?
- the family, her children, and extended family?
- her church experience?
- the financial situation?
- your work and her work situation?
- her involvement in society?
- her personal development?

I ask my wife these kinds of questions almost every year. This is a wonderful exercise to learn new perspectives and possibilities. I listen and write her answers down. Over the next few months, I talk with her about how she, God, and I could help her accomplish these ideas. As her husband, I benefit immensely from helping her achieve her life goals. It draws us together as we work on her becoming all she can become. Yes, there are constraints at times. Sometimes caring for the kids hold us back. Sometimes the lack of finances blocks us. Sometimes a lack of available time keeps her from pursuing something. But the fact that we both know the goal allows her to be patient and prepared for when the time is right. She knows I am for her.

One of the key goals for a husband is to help his wife fully develop. Unfortunately, many husbands have the idea that the wife should sacrifice all of her goals to help unfurl the husband's life and dreams. While a good wife will do this in her role as a wife, it is really the husband's role to do that for his wife as well (Ephesians 5:25–28). God almost assumes that the husband will develop and reach for his dreams. But He commands the gardener, the husband, to help his wife grow and produce her own unique fruit. So many marriages would be powerfully altered and blessed by a fuller development of the wife. The reason the woman's husband in Proverbs 31 is an elder and so well known is that his wife was so well developed. Her success benefitted him greatly.

Do you know what your wife's dreams, desires, and aspirations are for her life? What does she want to accomplish with the whole of her life? The first twenty years; the second twenty years; the third twenty years; the fourth twenty years; and even the fifth twenty years? As her husband, you get to help her achieve as many things as she can righteously achieve. When you learn what she wants to do, you can encourage, support, finance, pray for, and guide her to get there. Sometimes her dreams might need to wait a while until it's right for the family but assuring her that you will help her when the time is right goes a long way. When your wife feels the freedom to express her deepest desires, dreams, and goals, knowing you will back her, you will be fulfilling the Christ role in your marriage.

## Understand Her Temperament and Motivation Style

One of the most serious problems with many marriages is when the two people will not let each other be who they are. Quite often, people are attracted to and marry someone with a personality opposite to their own. These opposite tendencies are attractive at first but then can cause difficulties if each partner doesn't understand the differences. Just assume that your wife is wired completely different than you, and you're on your way. Once the marriage has been going on for a while, there is a natural desire to change the other person to act, think, and behave the way we want. This is a destructive tendency, and I see it in many failing marriages.

It is so helpful to understand your wife's personality and temperament, what motivates her, and what drains her. There are a vast number of resources you can use to determine this. Knowledge leads to greater understanding. I have listed a few I recommend here. See **Appendix 2** for more on temperament indicators.

Kiersey-Bates Temperament Sorter

Briggs-Meyer Personality Test

Strengthsfinder 2.0 by Tom Rath

The DISC Test

www.temperamentquiz.com

www.16personalities.com

www.discusonline.com

## Understand How She Gives and Receives Love

Have you ever thought you were expressing love to your wife only to have your message ignored or rebuffed? What you thought would get the point across went completely unnoticed. This happens in marriages all the time because people show and receive love in different ways. Sometimes your wife does not receive the messages of love you send and it can be completely baffling.

Author and psychologist Gary Chapman determined that we all tend to give and receive love in one of five ways, what he calls "love languages." It is important to realize that each person has his or her own preferred love language. We all tend to prefer one or two of them. This is significant because we will respond more quickly to messages of love that are sent in our preferred language. Messages sent in a different love language are often missed, ignored, or given a "that's nice" response.

This is a very powerful indicator of how much love is felt in your marriage. If you are giving love in a different language than your wife likes to receive, she may not understand the depth of what you are saying. **Appendix 3** summarizes the five love languages.[4]

### Growth Exercises—Take the Love Language Quiz

1. Determine your and your wife's love languages by taking a free, short quiz at **www.5lovelanguages.com**.

2. Spend a few minutes talking through and understanding some of the ways you both give and receive love.

# 6.

# HER NEED TO SEE YOU IMPROVE AND BECOME WISE OVER TIME

Susan had just done the unthinkable—she made a suggestion to her husband [gasp!]. In the past, Jim made his wife pay a high price for her constructive criticism. He belittled her, accused her of things she had done wrong, pointed out her weaknesses, attacked her family, and called her "a nag." His anger was emotionally intimidating. Eventually, the price was so high that she stopped making suggestions until one day when it really mattered.

Sue knew Jim had a lot of promise. He was extremely talented, but he was also his own worst enemy at times. If he was just willing to work on a few areas, she knew he could enjoy his fullest potential and a new level of success. She was hopeful for this particular upcoming opportunity.

Jim was interviewing for a new position at his present company. Susan was aware that he would not get the promotion unless he made some changes. She felt that he bragged too much about his accomplishments and skills. He needed to be more interested in the company and the owner rather than himself.

When Susan got up the courage to offer her suggestions for a successful interview, Jim argued with her and resisted her suggestions, even though he planned to do much of what she was saying. The more she talked, the angrier Jim became. Consequently, he changed his interview approach towards reflecting the pride and self-centeredness Susan was concerned about. "I'll show her!" he thought. He would run the interview his way—the very opposite way she suggested. It might come as no surprise that his unwillingness to listen to his wife cost him the promotion.

In another situation, Bill was consistently in a panic over projects because he did not get started on them until it was too late. He normally waited until the pressure of the deadline forced him to attempt something. In the earlier days of his marriage, his wife had lovingly suggested he start earlier on a needed repair or a new idea. His reaction was almost always the same, "Don't tell me what to do!"

Bill didn't realize that by "putting his woman in her place," he was about to lose his wife. She was already planning to divorce her husband emotionally, if not literally. Unfortunately, he was not interested in hearing about his impending doom. He was just not open to constructive criticism. His wife waited until the children were raised to leave him.

Part of understanding your wife realizes that she needs to see you become wiser and grow and mature over time. She is committed to being a partner to help you become fully successful in meeting life's challenges. She is aware of ideas, mannerisms, and perspectives that could make you supremely more effective in business and life. Most men make their wives pay a terrible price for trying to help. They are belittled, ignored, shouted down, intellectually dismissed, intimidated, or even physically threatened for trying to be helpful. Only when a man is willing to learn, be corrected, grow, and alter his plans will he accomplish the dreams he has hidden in his heart. The real question is, are you open to feedback that will help you?

## Growth Exercises—Where Does She Try to Add Value?

1. In what areas does your wife make suggestions?
   - Attire?
   - Business decisions?
   - Family conduct, what you spend your time doing, individual development?
   - Education?
   - Marital improvement?
   - Future?
   - Quality development?
   - Financial matters?
   - Other: _____

2. What is your general attitude toward her when she does this? Do you think she has your best interest in mind or not?

## Invite Growth and Correction

Most men resist their wives' rebuke or suggestions, leading to their own destruction. Their resistance causes them to miss out on two fronts—their wife's unique and helpful perspective that can bring more success in life and the importance of her participation. When a wife is not allowed to be a full helpmate to her husband, something begins to die in her relationship with him. She is not always aware that her respect and trust in him are diminishing. If you resist your wife's advice too many times, she will emotionally separate from you.

Most men can see this concept of rebuke at work. If a boss does not listen to suggestions from his employees, he will not be as successful. If he ignores criticism and new information, he chokes off avenues of success. Conversely, if a boss is open to suggestions, new ideas, and ways of doing things, it is a healthier work environment and more productive. If the boss is not open to input, the job will not usually hold a man's attention or loyalty.

A man *must* come to the place where he welcomes constructive criticism and asks where he can improve. This is how he can become what the Bible calls a "wise man." The more we welcome rebuke and instruction, the more of God's blessings we will enjoy. Our wives can help us reach our maximal potential and avoid the pitfalls that may destroy us; she wants to help, so let her. Try to give your wife permission to speak into your life to improve or redirect you. Invite opportunities for growth one time a month. More than that and it can feel too overwhelming.

The book of Proverbs is full of verses that instruct the wise man to seek out a rebuke and listen carefully to knowledge and instruction. I've listed some specific verses (NASB) below to read and reflect on.

---

"He is on the path of life who heeds instruction,
but he who forsakes reproof goes astray."

Proverbs 10:17

The word "life" carries the idea of an enjoyable, eventually, eternal life. This pathway requires that you be open to feedback. When you forsake the feedback you have heard, you wander from the path of life.

---

"Poverty and shame will come to him who neglects discipline,
but he who regards reproof will be honored."

Proverbs 13:18

Very few men aim at poverty and shame, but that is what they receive if they are unwilling to listen to the people God sends them to help. Swallow a little pride and get a better life. Ask your wife for one thing she might change about you to help you succeed. I usually ask my wife, "How do you see me limiting myself?"

---

"Stern discipline is for him who forsakes the way;
and he who hates reproof will die."

Proverbs 15:10

When you refuse to listen to others, God has stern discipline for you. He will not let His children run away from their fullest potential without a fight. When you fight against your wife's loving suggestions and corrections, you are, in a sense, forsaking God. If this stubbornness is not corrected, you will die without ultimately fulfilling your destiny.

---

"He whose ear listens to the life-giving reproof
will dwell among the wise. He who neglects discipline despises himself,
but he who listens to reproof acquires understanding."

Proverbs 15:31–32

This verse says that when husbands refuse to listen to their wives' criticisms, they are really destroying their own future. They despise themselves when they refuse to change or grow.

---

"Better is open rebuke than love that is concealed.
Faithful are the wounds of a friend, but deceitful
are the kisses of an enemy."

Proverbs 27:5

If you are not open to your wife's cautions, corrections, and feedback, she will conceal her love for you. When a friend is trying to point out how to succeed, you should listen even if it hurts.

# PRINCIPLE #3—SECURITY

"So husbands ought also to love
their own wives as their own bodies.
He who loves his own wife loves himself;
for no one ever hated his own flesh,
but nourishes and *cherishes* it,
just as Christ also does the church."

Ephesians 5:28–29 NASB (emphasis mine)

—⸮—

"She is gone again."

The voice on the other end of the line was familiar and sounded disheartened. Jack's wife had separated from him for the same general reasons as the time before. Eve was upset that he didn't have a steady job. She was fearful he was spending more money than he was making and felt intimidated whenever he got angry with her or the kids.

Jack had always been somewhat of a ladies' man, and Eve regularly accused him of having an affair. She had been reduced to tears regularly because of his ability to make every problem her fault. I had been counseling this couple for several years; they constantly separated and threatened divorce. He would be loving and caring to win back her love and trust, then destroy it. When she was secure about their relationship, there was no better marriage, but when she was insecure about the finances or his love, everything would slide downhill fast.

After repeated work and numerous failures, he began to make some progress.

Eventually, without realizing all he was doing, he got settled into a job and way of living that did not threaten his wife's security. This newfound security allowed their marriage to take root and flourish. After twenty years, they were doing better than at any point in the previous years.

Many men don't understand how their wife's stability level depends upon them. Men aren't naturally dependent creatures and don't constantly track the long-term future of their relationships. But this area of security is immense to a woman. Insecurity in the relationship makes it so that your wife cannot respond to you. A lack of security is a marriage killer if you don't deal with it.

When the average man is asked about his top five reasons for getting married, the answers usually include *respect, companionship,* and *sexual fulfillment.* Men rarely include security. When the average woman answers the question of why she got married, *security* is almost always in the top three. This idea of security branches into all kinds of security: emotional, physical, spiritual, mental, and financial.

To understand this need for security, I want you to picture a work environment. What would happen to your productivity at work if:

There is a rumor that the company is going to be sold.

Layoffs are coming, and there is no guarantee you are staying.

You had a poor performance review.

Others are now in the spotlight of favor at the company.

You don't know what the boss thinks about you and your work.

You have just been yelled at or embarrassed by your boss.

I'm willing to go out on a limb here and say that your security goes way, way down. This is the way many wives feel about their marriages. They are radically unsure of their security in the marriage. Your wife is constantly taking the temperature of the relationship. How are we doing financially? How are we doing emotionally? How are we doing spiritually? How are we doing physically? How are we doing sexually? Living in a threatening environment in any of these areas damages her ability to engage in the marriage fully.

## What Does It Take to Make Your Wife Feel Secure in the Marriage?

I have identified four primary "security areas" through countless counseling experiences with struggling couples. These four chapters will help you understand how a husband can build security in each area. These principles often turn the marriage around.

Chapter 7—Finances

Chapter 8—Anger

Chapter 9—Lust and Other Women

Chapter 10—Words

# 7.

## FINANCES

---

Paul wanted his marriage to succeed, but he was unaware of how his impulsive spending was destroying his marriage. When there wasn't enough money, he blamed his wife for what she spent on groceries. But Christy could not fix the family finances through the grocery budget. He blamed her for their financial difficulties. When we sat down and looked at the actual expenses and patterns of spending, it was clear his impulsive spending was dooming the family, not hers. In Paul's case, he purchased a van he had always wanted "for his family." The payment for the van was almost $600 a month. His impulse to impress his family and friends completely sunk the finances and put their marriage at risk.

It took us a while and a good amount of learning to get Paul and Christy on solid financial footing. They had to return the van. They had to work together to set the budget. They had to agree before they bought things. They needed to explore new streams of income. Paul was able to rebuild his marriage and his wife's security by rebuilding the family's financial picture. In spite of the mess he had made with the finances, their marriage survived and even thrived as he developed new levels of financial security.

If your wife does not feel secure in the relationship, she cannot respond the way you need her to. It does not do any good to demand she not worry about the money. She sees the financial situation as an integral part of the strength of the marriage. It is the husband's job to make the marriage financially stable and communicate his ideas to her so they can be on the same page. He does not have to handle, control, or even make all the money, but he is responsible for the financial situation within the family. I've listed below some principles and actions that will allow you to put your family finances in order and set your wife at ease.

## How to Build Financial Stability and Security for Your Family

How can a husband improve his marriage by creating financial security for his family? By following sound biblical advice in the area of money. There are a few basic principles you need to learn and master. Let me recommend that both husband and wife attend a Financial Peace University seminar together. I will go over these basic biblical ideas here in this chapter, but attending the actual seminar will help you practice these ideas. For more information about a seminar near you, visit www.daveramsey.com.

*Get out of unsecured debt. (Proverbs 6:1–5)*

Have a discussion with your wife about eliminating debt. Start from the smallest debt and work toward the biggest. Start from the highest interest rate debt to the lowest interest rate debt. By following a disciplined plan, the debt in your family can be paid off. When your wife sees you are serious about putting your family on firm financial footing, her security will grow and she will respond to you.

One of the greatest investors in America, Warren Buffet, is regularly asked how to get started on the road to building wealth. He first asks the person if they have any credit card debt. If the person says "yes," he tells them the first step is to pay off that debt. Nothing he could tell them to do would produce more than the 18 to 20 percent interest they are losing through that debt.

If you have debt, develop a serious plan to pay it off. There are many different good plans, but let me suggest the debt-reducing snowball plan. This is where you list all of your debt in order from lowest to highest. You list the minimum payment for each. Then see if there is any way to add more to the lowest debt payment and try and pay it off. When that is paid off, add the amount you were paying for that smallest debt to the next smallest debt. Add that amount to the third smallest debt when that debt is paid off. I have watched a couple pay off $83,000 in debt using this method. It is amazing how paying off debt alleviates stress in the marriage.

*Understand your financial position and make a budget. (Proverbs 27:23–27)*

Many men believe the finances will take care of themselves. They think they do not need to know where the money goes or how much they have at any given point in time. However, since the state of your finances often reflects the security of your wife in the relationship, it is crucial that you, as the husband, understand the financial condition of your family. You need to know what bills will be coming up and the various obligations of your family. You do not necessarily need to keep the records yourself, but you must understand what is happening with your family's finances. Have a good record-keeping system and interact with your wife on the bills and coming purchases.

One of the most helpful ways of making a budget is by starting with the general categories and the typical percentages that are healthy in those categories. Here are some guidelines:

- 40% of budget on your mortgage or rent payment.
- 15% on groceries.
- 6% to 10% on recreation and entertainment.
- 6% on miscellaneous spending.
- 6% to 10% on debt service (beyond housing payment).

There are a series of great computer programs to install on your phone or computer to help you work through all budget categories. I recommend learning how to budget through Financial Peace University but using You Need a Budget (YNAB) as a budgeting tool. Seeing where every dollar is going before you spend anything is very powerful. Many people make the mistake of looking at their bank balance to see if they have money to spend. But usually, all the money in your bank account is already committed to bills coming due. If you learn to work with your wife on making a reasonable family budget, it will help your marriage avoid the typical ups and downs. I have found that usually, within two weeks to six months, most couples can stop living paycheck-to-paycheck. Step up and learn how to have a family budget that promotes security.

*Spend less than you make every month.*

Way too many people spend everything they make every month. Biblical counsel suggests we spend between 50 to 70 percent of our income and save, invest, and give the remainder. Set aside these savings first and live on the rest. A number of years ago I had a financial planner tell me, in no uncertain terms, "This is what you should be saving for retirement." So I started with the tithe to God, then I set aside what he said I should be saving for retirement. I then set aside another amount for my emergency fund and another amount to give to various charities to help the poor. Our family lived on what was left. This was the point when we started to get healthy financially. Every week I know we are living within our means. Every week I know I am saving for the future. Every week I know I am building security into my wife's life financially. She knows she can count on me not to get to the end of our working years and have nothing to live on. She knows she can count on me to strengthen our family's financial health every month.

This idea is based loosely on some ancient Jewish wisdom woven into God's command for a "poor tithe" in the books of Exodus and Deuteronomy. It encourages spending only 50 percent of your income and using the rest for financial health personally and societally. The "poor tax" was a second tithe on your income given to the poor each year. The idea meant that Jewish households would divide their income—50 percent for expenses, 10 percent for tithe to God, 20 percent for investments, 10 percent for the poor, 10 percent for an emergency fund. This builds security both personally and societally. At first, it requires sacrifice as you are living on a lot less than what you have in the past, but it quickly brings new financial health and financial freedom. Of course, you don't have to follow this idea as we are not under the law; it is another way of dividing your income.

Many people have found that spending 70 percent on expenses, 10 percent on the tithe, 10 percent on investment, and 10 percent on an emergency fund is a perfect place to start and less stark. Whatever you and your spouse decide to do, do it together and get away from thinking that you spend everything you make. It is your job as a husband to help your marriage and family have a reasonable plan to build financial health for the present and the future. Again, let me say there are great courses like Financial Peace University from Dave Ramsey that can get you started on a much healthier financial future.

*Give tithes and offerings to the Lord. (Malachi 3:8–11 and Matthew 6:19–24)*

The Lord will bless Christians who honor the Lord from their income in many areas of life. God tells us that if we honor Him with tithes and offerings, He will throw open up the windows of heaven and shower upon us His blessings until there is no more need. It is incredible how often God works powerfully in a family's life after they begin the process of tithing to their local church.

I can remember talking with my father about how my mother started tithing before he became a Christian. He wanted to get upset at her, but he noticed that money poured into their checking account from new sources that more than made up for the part she gave away. He told me it was weird to see the budget consistently work even when it shouldn't. He knew something miraculous was taking place, even though he wasn't ready to believe in God back then.

I highly recommend discussing how to become generous by giving tithes and offerings to the Lord. This discussion may take several weeks and months before you actually move in this direction. If either of you is hesitant, try an experiment where you will tithe to the church you attend for six weeks and see if God does not bless you in numerous ways and allow your budget to work. God even says to test Him in this area of bringing in the whole tithe in Malachi 3:10. He can be trusted in this area of finances.

These are just a few financial principles that will allow your family to be financially free and stable. Economic freedom and stability may take a while to develop, but it is worth the time and energy. Here are some great resources I recommend.

*Financial Peace University*
(ramseysolutions.com) and
*Total Money Makeover*
by Dave Ramsey

You Need A Budget
(youneedabudget.com),
YNAB app

*The Principle of Maximums*
by Roger Stichter

*Managing God's Money*
by Randy Alcorn

*How to Manage Your Money*
by Larry Burkett

*The Millionaire Next Door*
by Thomas Stanley and
William Danko

# 8.

## ANGER

———

**M**any of us men have a problem with anger. Uncontrolled or undisciplined anger is one of the great marriage dividers. We don't understand that when we get angry, even if it is not directed at our wives, it threatens her security. Anger is primarily a result of unrealistic expectations. When something doesn't happen the way we want or in the time frame we expect, that is when anger flairs. Our expectations were unrealistic for that situation, that amount of communication, that amount of time, and so forth. Our wives need to see that we don't always have to get our way and that we can control our temper.

I remember soon after my wife and I got married, I smacked my head on a desk while trying to hang wallpaper—yes, I got angry. I came out from under the desk hurt, angry, and frustrated. I had this habit—whenever I got hurt—of clenching my fist, gritting my teeth, and growling. I thought it was a good way of not punching something. Dana immediately started backing away from me. I could see she was afraid, so I moved toward her and snarled, "I'm not angry at you." This did not help.

It took some time for us to be able to talk about this incident. She said it didn't matter if I was angry at her or not, just that I was angry. In those types of situations, I wasn't managing my anger well. Of course, she was right, and I began a new level of anger management. When I was single, my anger worked fine, but now as a married man, I needed a new level of control and understanding to build security in my wife.

After careful study, I came up with four Anger Management Strategies (AMS) from the scriptures that work for me. They help me express less anger when I am hurt, and they have helped many men and women I've counseled deal with their anger, frustration, and irritations. I believe they will work for you too. It is important to have a proven strategy in place to prevent you from slipping into short-lived fits of rage, which can quickly destroy all you hope for in the marriage.

## AMS One—Reason (Ephesians 4:25–5:2)

This strategy depends on using reason to understand where anger comes from, what it is, and what it will become if it is not managed well. First, we need to understand emotions. Emotions are energy to do various things. Without emotions, life is drab and dull. With both good and bad emotions, life has energy, passion, joy, and, vitality. But too many people think that if you are a good Christian, you will not have strong emotions. Nothing could be further from the truth. Just take a trip through the psalms and you will see all kinds of emotions being expressed while worshipping God. We are emotional creatures, and we need emotions to fuel our lives.

Often, emotion, in its rawest form, is too strong. For emotions to be useful, they need to be processed and aimed at the right actions. For example, love powers commitment and sacrifice; sadness powers grief and mourning; joy powers positivity and relational bonding; anger powers change.

All unrighteous anger begins as an emotional reaction to not getting your way. It is addictive and a powerful emotional drug. It is not considered sin until you embrace and express it in an unrighteous way (Ephesians 4:26). Anger is sinfully expressed in six ways (Colossians 3:8):

Bitterness—the putrid smell stewing in your heart

Wrath—mad at the world

Anger—irritated at one person, pleasant to others

Clamor—the volcano, the screamer

Slanderer—the devil tongue, spitting cobra

Malice—the vengeance factor

To be angry and not sin means we must refine our angry emotions, just as raw crude oil must be refined into gasoline, kerosene, plastics, jet fuel, and the like. When refined and processed, righteous anger can bring about positive change in our life, our family, and our community. What could our anger fuel? If we are going to live a successful life, build a great marriage, or enjoy a rewarding career, we will have to change the way we act, our reactions, the way we speak (words and tone), and our attitude.

Don't just let raw fuel spill out of you constantly. Use it for good purposes to become a better person.

## AMS Two—Reset Expectations
## (Proverbs 19:11; Philippians 4:8)

One of the most helpful truths about anger is that much of it comes from wishes or desires that have hardened into unrealistic expectations. Most of the time, it comes from selfishness, lack of leadership, or a boundary issue. I am deeply indebted to my mentor, Gary Smalley, for pointing out this connection between expectations and anger. If I am angry, then I most likely have an unrealistic expectation about something. If I am angry because drivers won't get out of my way on the freeway, it's because I am being selfish. If I expect my wife to read my mind, things won't go well because I'm not communicating well. If I teach my children how to do something, expecting they will do it perfectly after that, my lack of leadership and unrealistic expectations won't get me the results I'm looking for.

The next time you get angry, ask yourself if it is reasonable to expect what you expect to happen? If you are angry, the answer is always *no*. Many of us expect others to automatically do the things we want them to do the way we want them to, but this is unrealistic. We need to reset our expectations, communicate clearly, and lead them better. This takes planning, allotting more time, being nicer, and being clear about directions. It may be that our expectations will never happen for various reasons, so we need to keep them as hopes, dreams, and desires rather than expectations.

There is a lot of work to be done before our wishes, dreams, and desires can become reality. That is where the energy from anger comes in. If you can refine the energy in your frustration into actual positive planning, then change can happen. But spewing your demands and selfishness onto others will not produce the kind of change you want. Even if the other person does what you want, your anger damages the relationship. Apologize if you have vomited your anger on the people around you.

Many men allow their ego to harden their desires into unrealistic expectations. In other words, they believe they should get everything they want. Instead of being mad at your wife or kids, ask God how you should be viewing things. What is the realistic expectation? What should your attitude be for this situation? How can you best lead them? Instead of being angry at your boss for not giving you a promotion or a raise, ask what you could do to make sure you get the promotion next time. Some men are mad for days about what they want to happen. I usually counsel men that if they are angry, it means they have an unrealistic expectation. If this sounds like you, admit that your expectation may be unrealistic and take it back down to a wish, hope, or desire.

## AMS Three—Play Dead (Proverbs 17:14; Romans 6:11)

This strategy is based upon the idea of playing dead or being non-responsive to the "voice" of anger inside of you. You can choose to do something different from what the anger wants you to do. It is based on the idea contained in Romans 6:11, "Even so consider yourself dead to sin, but alive to God in Christ Jesus." The idea here is that when your flesh (selfishness) is speaking, the Holy Spirit is also whispering what to do instead of letting anger take control. If you pause and don't respond to the impulses of anger, and instead, ask God for what He wants you to do and then do it, you will beat the temptation.

I have found that I do not have long where I can remain in this non-responsive state. Often it is less than two minutes before I need to start doing what the Holy Spirit suggests to beat the temptation. After you have beaten the temptation, you can examine where it came from. Trying to examine the motives and reasons for anger at the moment is often too much even for the most seasoned saint.

## AMS Four—Love (Matthew 5:43; Luke 6:27–36; Galatians 2:20)

This strategy depends on using the force of God's love to choke out anything not of Him, in this case, unrighteous anger. We can inject love and positive actions toward another person to battle against anger. Try this strategy for yourself and see the difference it makes. When a person or situation consistently brings irritation, frustration, or anger in your life, it means you need to enact more love there to drown out the anger. When your spouse is not responding to your ideas, plans, or actions, ask God how you can love her more (meet her needs, pursue her, please her) rather than get angry with her.

Jesus tells us how to treat those we think are opposing us in Luke 6:27–36 (NASB):

---

But I say to you who hear, love your enemies, do good to those who hate you, bless those who curse you, pray for those who mistreat you. Whoever hits you on the cheek, offer him the other also; and whoever takes away your coat, do not withhold your shirt from him either. Give to everyone who asks of you, and whoever takes away what is yours, do not demand it back. Treat others the same way you want them to treat you. If you love those who love you, what credit is that to you? For even sinners love those who love them. If you do good to those who do good to you, what credit is that to you? For even sinners do the same. If you lend to those from whom you expect to receive, what credit is that to you? Even sinners lend to sinners in order to receive back the same amount. But love your enemies, and do good, and lend, expecting nothing in return; and your reward will be great, and you will be sons of the Most High; for He Himself is kind to ungrateful and evil men. Be merciful, just as your Father is merciful.

———

In this example, ask God:

How can I bless the irritating person?

How can I pray for the person who is persecuting me?

How can I do good to the person who is using me?

How, in what way, and when should I love my enemies?

Directly increase my love for the other person.

Show me how to meet their real needs so that I can overcome the irritating aspects of dealing with them.

Give me Your love for this person.

Tell God you are willing to rent your body to Jesus for Him to love this person through you. Galatians 2:20 (NASB) says, "I have been crucified with Christ; and it is no longer I who live, but Christ lives in me; and the life which I now live in the flesh I live by faith in the Son of God, who loved me and gave Himself up for me." God calls us to love one another, and He will help us do this seemingly impossible task if we ask Him.

As for your wife, ask God how He wants to love her through your body, words, attitudes, and listening. This assignment has saved so many families. If you will let Jesus love your spouse through you, I think you'll find how much you really love her.

# 9.

## LUST AND OTHER WOMEN

The one action that damages a marriage more quickly and deeply than almost any other is uncontrolled lust. Whether lust breaks out into an affair or simmers beneath the surface through pornography, it is deadly to the bonds of marriage.

Most men do not understand how damaging it is to compare their wives to other women in an unfavorable way. Remember, your wife needs to know she is number one in your heart. You looking at other women definitely threatens her security. She needs to sense she has a permanent and primary place of honor in your soul. You lose if you compare your wife to other women or lift other women as better than her.

Pornography, flirting, affairs, or mental fantasies barge into a woman's life with the message: "You can't compete!" "You lose!" "I may be gone at any time!" These are devastating messages to send. There is no way a woman can fully respond sexually or emotionally to a man who has already "told" her that she is subpar. And it is my conviction that a woman receives these destructive messages in her spirit whether or not her husband's secret lust life has yet been brought to the light.

I remember visiting with one man whose wife was a very attractive lady who had lived a rough life before she became a Christian. She was incensed that her husband would look at other women. If she caught him looking at other women, she would slug him right in the jaw!

He told me about a time when he was walking down the street and talking with his wife. He spied a good-looking lady out of the corner of his eye. He knew from experience that he could not turn his head because his wife would know what he was doing. He just kept his head straight and watched with his eyes. He walked straight into a pole on the sidewalk! After he hit the pole, his wife figured out why he did not see the pole and slugged him. This is a dramatic example of what happens when a strong woman sees her husband involved with lust, but you get the idea.

A wife needs her husband to have eyes only for her. "Why can't you be like so and so?" is a deadly combination of words. Even when a man points out the strong points of another woman, his wife is usually thinking, "What does he think about me in this area?"

If you want a strong marriage, your wife must implicitly trust that she is the one and only woman in your life. It helps to follow up any positive comment about other women with a note that your wife is stronger or in some way more competent or alluring than this other individual. In terms of beauty, your wife is the only woman with whom you can have sexual relations without actual guilt before a holy God. Therefore, by definition, she is the most beautiful woman on the planet.

She needs to know you have, *by an act of the will,* fixed your focus on one woman—her. Other women are in some other category. They exist, but they aren't alluring or potential companions, and they certainly don't compete with her.

## Overcoming Lust

Embracing lust includes when you have mentally entered into a fantasy about or with another woman. It also includes when you have taken steps to fulfill your sexual pleasure with another woman and when you may have wanted to satisfy a sexual desire but were blocked by various obstacles. These are sinful embraces of strong desire or lust. The Bible is clear about what happens when we indulge in lust. It leads to sin and ruin.

If you would like to work through a deeper discussion of this subject with many more solutions and techniques, my book and online class, *Mission Possible: Winning the Battle over Temptation,* can help you do this (www.udemy.com). I hope you'll check it out if you need it or refer it to others you know of that need help in this area.

Here are four basic steps that can lead you to victory in overcoming lust.

### Step One—Confess when you've given in to temptations to lust.

To overcome lust, we need to immediately admit when we have embraced thoughts of lust. It is very helpful for men who struggle in this area of sexual temptation (and many do, believe me) to be a part of an accountability partnership with others who also struggle in this area. This could be a group of men, a trusted friend, or a mentor to talk to within a safe setting. In some cases, it is helpful to bring your wife into the accountability process.

Please note that it is not sinful to have had a sexual thought that you did not embrace or act upon. It is also not a sin to enjoy sexual fantasy with your wife (within moral limits). God has given us a strong desire for sexual pleasure and gave you an authorized outlet for that desire—your wife. Exercise your imagination in the direction of your spouse. However, train your imagination to not move in the direction of other people in the sexual arena.

Do not coddle your sin by excusing it or hiding it. If you are involved in embracing lust, then it is sin. You will not be able to conquer it until you admit that what you are involved in is wrong.

---

"For the free gift of eternal salvation is now being offered to everyone; and along with this gift comes the realization that God wants us to turn from godless living and sinful pleasures and to live good, God-fearing lives day after day."

Titus 2:11–12 TLB

---

"If we confess our sins, He is faithful and just to forgive us our sins and to cleanse us from all unrighteousness."

1 John 1:9 ESV

---

*Step Two—Eliminate anything that encourages or stimulates lust in you.*

This would certainly include any involvement with temptation via computers, iPads, books, music, TV, movies, magazines, friends, situations, jobs, and so forth. Here are some verses that underline this theme:

---

"You have heard that it was said, 'You shall not commit adultery.' But I say to you that everyone who looks at a woman with lust for her has already committed adultery with her in his heart. If your right eye makes you stumble, tear it out and throw it from you; for it is better for you to lose one of the parts of your body, than for your whole body to be thrown into hell."

Matthew 5:27–29 ESV

———

"Be decent and true in everything you do so that all can approve your behavior. Don't spend your time in wild parties and getting drunk or in adultery and lust or fighting or jealousy. But ask the Lord Jesus Christ to help you live as you should, and don't make plans to enjoy evil."

Romans 13:12–14 TLB

———

"Run from anything that gives you the evil thoughts that young men often have but stay close to anything that makes you want to do right. Have faith and love and enjoy the companionship of those who love the Lord and have pure hearts."

2 Timothy 2:22–24 TLB

———

There is a wise old saying: "Others may; you cannot." While some people can handle certain activities and actions, they may be serious temptations for you that move you toward sin. It is not possible to judge the righteousness of an activity, thing, or action based upon who else is able to enjoy it. It is between you and the Holy Spirit.

You have to get a handle on the influences in your life. Make a serious evaluation of what moves you toward sin and seek to eliminate that from your life. Only when you come to terms with the myriad of influences in your life will you be able to overcome certain sins.

Do not have an "I-can-handle-it" attitude. When something regularly produces lust in your life, eliminate it. Don't think you should be able to handle it. While there are some circumstances that require a person to get stronger, the majority of the influences that produce lust should be eliminated.

Also, I might add that when you are in a family or group context, whoever is the most sensitive to a particular influence should be the one who decides what is eliminated or retained. Just because one person is strong and likes a particular activity does not mean the activity should be retained. If one of the members of the group is regularly tripped up by the activity, action, or situation, then it should be eliminated from the group. Examples of this are violent or sexually explicit TV shows or movies, but it could also be exposure to certain people or hangouts.

*Step Three—Renew your mind through biblical meditation.*

Ephesians 6:12–20 tells us about using the spiritual weapons God has provided us to do battle against evil. Verse 17 says to use the sword of the Spirit, the word of God, to do battle whenever temptation attacks. Listed below are some very powerful verses to look up and write down on a piece of paper and commit to memory. These will be invaluable to you as temptation comes at you. It takes time to do this, but believe through faith that it is time wisely spent and will work when you need it.

## Key Temptation Verses

| | |
|---|---|
| Ps. 119:10,11 | Rom. 6:1–14,16 |
| 1 Thess. 4:1–9 | Rom. 8:1–14 |
| Col. 3:1–10,16 | Ps. 19:14 |
| 1 Cor. 3:11–20 | Ps. 1:2,3 |
| 1 Cor. 10:12–15 | Jas. 1:1–8,13 |
| 2 Cor. 10:3–5 | Gal. 5:16–6:5 |
| Heb. 12:1–17 | Col. 3:14–16 |
| | 1 Pet. 4:1–3 |

*Step Four—Instantly obey the promptings of the Holy Spirit.*

Scripture says we are to be anxious to do the will of God (1 Peter 4:2 TLB). To have victory over lust, you must be prepared to instantly submit to the subtle promptings of the Holy Spirit. The Holy Spirit knows what is coming and will alert you to do something different to head off a path that leads to strong temptations. Many men have ignored the gentle nudges of the Spirit of God and have proceeded to act on the temptation to their peril. God always has the antidote for lust, but we must take it before the disease takes root in our lives. The antidote is almost always doing something righteous instead of the lascivious alternative.

———

"Do not let sin control your puny body any longer;
do not give in to its sinful desires. Do not let any part of your bodies
become tools of wickedness, to be used for sinning;
but give yourselves completely to God—every part of you."

Romans 6:12–13a TLB

———

"I advise you to obey only the Holy Spirit's instructions.
He will tell you where to go and what to do, and then you won't always
be doing the wrong things your evil nature wants you to…
But when you follow your own wrong inclinations your lives will produce
these evil results: impure thoughts, eagerness for lustful pleasure."

Galatians 5:16,18 TLB

———

Having self-control means you are ready and responding to the promptings of the Holy Spirit. It is not possible to have victory in this area without the direct leadership of the Holy Spirit. God knows how to keep us out of the areas, situations, and circumstances that will be too strong for us. Remember that when lust is tempting you, the Holy Spirit is also prompting you. If you are not careful, lust will drown out the movement of the Holy Spirit upon your heart.

## Growth Exercises—Defeating Lust in Your Life

1.  Review the steps above and decide which one you most need to work on.

    - Do you need to get rid of anything in your home or at work that provokes lust in you?

    - Do you need to ask some men to get together once a week for accountability?

    - Do you need to start right away memorizing those Scripture verses?

    - What hidden temptation zones do you need to identify and flush out of your life?

2.  Go deeper by signing up for the online video course, *Mission Possible: Winning the Battle over Temptation,* which can be accessed on Udemy.com or by scanning the QR code below.

    Take each lesson seriously as you practice each exercise. You can also get a copy of the print book by the same name that provides even more instruction and exercises. Don't hesitate to get the help you need.

**Mission Possible: Winning the Battle over Temptation**
Online course at Udemy.com

# 10.

# WORDS

---

**A**n area where your wife is very sensitive is your words about her and towards her. Your words allow her to gauge the stability of the relationship. Words are powerful; we know this. So as her husband, do everything you can to use what you say to build unshakeable stability in your marriage.

There are enough outside pressures and problems that can destabilize your marriage, so work hard not to have your words perform "an inside job." Positive words can help your wife understand that you are committed to the relationship, love her, and that everything will be okay. It would help if you regularly verbalized phrases, ideas, and comments to build her security, not tear it down. Look at what Scripture says about the power of the tongue:

> For we all stumble in many ways. If anyone does not stumble in what
> he says, he is a perfect man, able to bridle the whole body as well.
> Now if we put the bits into the horses' mouths so that they will obey us,
> we direct their entire body as well. Look at the ships also, though they are
> so great and are driven by strong winds, are still directed by a very small
> rudder wherever the inclination of the pilot desires. So also the tongue
> is a small part of the body, and yet it boasts of great things.
>
> See how great a forest is set aflame by such a small fire!
> And the tongue is a fire, the very world of iniquity; the tongue is set
> among our members as that which defiles the entire body, and sets on fire
> the course of our life, and is set on fire by hell. For every species of beasts
> and birds, of reptiles and creatures of the sea, is tamed and has been tamed

by the human race. But no one can tame the tongue; it is a restless evil
and full of deadly poison. With it we bless our Lord and Father,
and with it we curse men, who have been made in the likeness of God;
from the same mouth come both blessing and cursing.
My brethren, these things ought not to be this way. Does a fountain
send out from the same opening both fresh and bitter water?
Can a fig tree, my brethren, produce olives, or a vine produce figs?
Nor can salt water produce fresh.

James 3:2–12 NASB

---

## The Power to Build Up or Destroy

The following list, while common, produces disastrous results for a wife's sense of security. In other words, **never say these kinds of things...**

# Do Not Say These Things!

I don't know whether this relationship will work out.

Maybe I shouldn't have married you.

Being married to you is okay; it's just your family I can't stand.

Do you ever think about what it would be like
if we weren't married?

How could you do that? I can't believe I have such a stupid wife.

I give up. I guess I have to do that (responsibility), too.

What have you been doing? Are you completely useless?

Maybe we should get a divorce.

Maybe you should spend some time with your mother.

Never curse at your wife or call her a derogatory name.

I'm sure you can see that if the same words were said to you, they would at the very least raise an eyebrow, but for her, they are devastating. In contrast, here are examples of security-building phrases you should say all the time:

# Say These Things!

When I married you, I couldn't wait to be with you, but now I also realize that I can't do without you.

I enjoy being with you.

We make a good team.

I like working through problems with you.

We come up with good solutions together.

I was at work today, and I just caught myself thinking about you.

I more and more realize how right God was to pick you for me.

I can't wait to grow old with you.

I'm so happy I married you, and I would do it again.

When you say these kinds of phrases throughout the marriage, trust and security take root and blossom. The Bible mentions the tongue and our speech many, many times. God knows how easily we can build up or destroy with our words. It behooves you as a husband, father, and man of God to learn to exercise self-control with your tongue and use your words to edify and build up the people in your life.

## Growth Exercises—Build Her Security by Taming the Tongue

Write down a few security-oriented statements that communicate your commitment to your wife that could allay any insecurities she may have. Speak at least one of these statements into her life every day. This is not praise, necessarily. It is a statement that makes her feel secure in the relationship.

Here are some excellent principles for taming the tongue and the verses that go with them. I recommend memorizing these verses and putting them on little cards you carry in your pocket. Please read them over and over again until they are in your head. The Holy Spirit will bring them to mind when you need to say something different than what you probably want to say.

### There is incredible power in words.

"Death and life are in the power of the tongue,
and those who love it will eat its fruits."
Proverbs 18:21

### Give a gentle answer.

"A gentle answer turns away wrath,
but a harsh word stirs up anger.
A soothing tongue is a tree of life,
but perversion in it crushes the spirit."
Proverbs 15:1,4

### Offer an apt answer.

"A man has joy in an apt answer,
and how delightful is a timely word!"
Proverbs 15:23

### Guard your mouth.

"He who guards his mouth and his tongue,
guards his soul from troubles."
Proverbs 21:23

### Keep silent.

"Even a fool, when he keeps silent, is considered wise;
when he closes his lips, he is considered prudent."
Proverbs 17:28

### Be slow to speak.

"Do you see a man who is hasty in his words?
There is more hope for a fool than for him."
Proverbs 29:20

### Halt careless words.
"But I tell you that every careless word
that people speak,
they shall give an accounting for it
in the day of judgment."
Matthew 12:36

### Offer edifying words.
"Let no unwholesome word proceed from your mouth,
but only such a word as is good for edification
according to the need of the moment,
so that it will give grace to those who hear."
Ephesians 4:29

### Be slow to speak angrily.
"But everyone must be quick to hear,
slow to speak and slow to anger;
for the anger of man does not achieve
the righteousness of God."
James 1:19, 20

### Bridle your tongue.
"If anyone thinks himself to be religious,
and yet does not bridle his tongue
but deceives his own heart,
this man's religion is worthless."
James 1:26

### Refrain from evil speech.
"For, 'The one who desires life,
to love and see good days,
must keep his tongue from evil
and his lips from speaking deceit.'"
1 Peter 3:10

## Final Thoughts about Security

Let me tell you the story of Mark and Janice. Mark needed Janice when they first met and when they got married. Janice was amazing and beautiful. She gave Mark so much confidence and encouragement that this put his life on a track to success. His growth and prospects for the future were literally amazing. He knew it was because of Janice.

Somewhere after the first few years of marriage, Mark began to let his negativity leak out onto Janice. He used the confidence she had given him to put her down. He went back to handling his money in an undisciplined fashion. He took needless risks and bought impulsively. He flashed his old anger patterns, screaming and yelling at her when he was angry at others. He compared her to other women when they made love and belittled her in front of others. Everyone knew she was amazing, including Mark, but he just let his old habits dominate the way he treated her.

Sure enough, over a few years, he emotionally and spiritually pummeled her into a shadow of herself. Then he blamed her for the fact that she could not be everything for him like before. He eventually divorced her after he destroyed her. She is rebuilding her life without him, while he is wandering in the darkness created by his own choices. Build your wife up and create a secure environment for your marriage so that the two of you can grow old together and be best friends. Don't do what Mark did and wind up alone without the love of his life.

As we have discussed, these areas of security really do threaten your wife's sense of how the marriage is going. She cannot continue to respond to you if you allow these areas to exist unchecked in your life. I hope you will actually do the projects outlined in each chapter. Without the work, you will not realize the maximum benefit from this information and teaching.

Your wife will immediately notice your improvement in these areas. Go ahead and begin working on them—make some improvements first before asking for forgiveness for all the wrongs of the past. She will forgive you if you are sincere and can see changes being made. Remember, your wife is counting on you to develop security and not to destroy it. You can do this!

# PRINCIPLE #4—BUILDING UNITY

"For this reason a man shall leave his father and his mother, and be joined to his wife; and they shall become one flesh."

Genesis 2:24 NASB

∞

**H**is wife came at him hard and fast. He was the problem for this latest disaster in the family, and she was giving him an earful about his failings. Usually, he fired back at her with equal fury about how she was the problem, and if she had only done this or that, the problem would not have happened. But this time, he decided to just listen to her rant about how he had really blown it.

As he allowed her to get it all out, he fought off the desire to correct her and point out where she was the problem. He could even see that she could be right. Instead of blowing up, he asked himself this crucial question: "If I fire back and prove to her that she is the problem or divert attention away from how I have blown it, will that make our marriage stronger or fix the problem?" The answer was clearly *no*!

For the first time, he saw that if he were drawn into an argument, there would be no way to make the marriage better in relation to this problem. He had to lead in a completely different way than he had in the past. There had to be another way of handling problems and difficulties—a better way than arguing about them or giving in to her completely.

There is another way. It is called *building unity*, the topic of this chapter. Your leadership as the husband must pull the couple together, not dominate with your way of thinking. God has called you to wise leadership in the home where everybody wins. You will not win a great marriage if you constantly demand your own way. Instead, you must work with your wife to lead you both to a better place—a better marriage. Sometimes this means you have to listen to her corrective ideas, and that's okay. In business, a boss who is not open to suggestions or corrective criticism is not a good leader.

Building unity is leadership at a higher level. The lowest level of leadership is forcing your spouse to do it your way. The highest levels of leadership include providing a vision for a unified future. Remember, if you get what you want, but your spouse hates you, you have not won.

A life full of love requires sharing your unique perspectives and pursuing goals together. God calls husbands to lead through wisdom, vision, and building unity. This means bringing the wonder of both of your perspectives into wise goals, decisions, and plans where everyone wins.

God says that when a man and woman marry, they are no longer two people, but they become one flesh (Ephesians 5:31). It is not a good thing when your arm tries to do its own thing in rebellion against the other parts of the body. Something is dangerously wrong when your liver rebels and refuses to do its crucial function.

Becoming one flesh involves more than just the act of physical intercourse. Becoming one flesh means that two people begin to move and think as one unit. While the two individuals still exist, there is a oneness of purpose, direction, and action that demonstrates unity.

A wife wants to believe that her husband is for their marriage, not just himself. She needs evidence that you will fight for a goal you didn't even care about before you were married. All wives need to be in harmony and unity with their husbands. Too often, a husband destroys her trust by selfish, arbitrary, or impulsive decisions. You can become the godly man she wants you to be. What changes are needed to unify your marriage rather than two selfish individuals living together? It is clear from scripture that man is to take the initiative in developing this unity (Ephesians 5:25; 1 Corinthians 11:3).

Before Brian was married, he could do what he pleased with his days off, but now that he is married to Ashley, he needs to talk, plan, and consider options with Ashley. His goal is no longer simply, "What do I want to do?" His leadership must include what Ashley wants to do and what will cause the marriage to thrive. As he understands what it means to build unity, he wins more than what he wants. Brian wins delightful, intimate interactions with Ashley. Brian wins new perspectives and emotional growth. Brian becomes a much better young man because his leadership is aimed at more than just himself.

The tragedy of many marriages is that they become a business relationship over time. It is always the same path: the distance grows between people as they pursue what they personally want. Someone must lead the couple out of this wilderness of selfishness. God has put that responsibility on you, the husband. Think of larger goals. Sacrifice some immediate desires for bigger gains down the road. Husbands must engage in this unity work to make it happen.

Building unity and closeness requires listening, discussing, praying, and being open to ideas. I can remember many discussions my wife and I had that started with her wanting a different vacuum or a different car or a different vacation than I wanted. Then through the miracle of me staying engaged and her increased flexibility, we came up with solutions we had never considered before. She often came up with a new great idea, and sometimes I did. Sometimes it was her parents, a friend of ours, or a wise person we checked with. My job was to lead with an openness that resulted in wisdom we could both get behind.

Look for wisdom. It will become obvious when you find it. When a wife sees that a husband wants wisdom above his own way, she will ensure that the husband gets to have their hobby, sport, game, or fun. But the first idea that allows her to relax is, "Does this man I am married to want to find wisdom or just his way?" Remember, you may want unity and harmony, but your wife *needs* unity and harmony.

## What Is Involved in Building Unity?

In the following three chapters, we will look at three ways to build unity into your marriage:

Chapter 11—Find and Face the Common Enemy

Chapter 12—Enjoy Shared Experiences

Chapter 13—Protect Your Wife's Weaknesses

# 11.

# FIND AND FACE THE COMMON ENEMY

---

The natural process of marriage is for the man and the woman to slip into roles that separate them and cause them to feel like they are living in different worlds. This process can eventually lead a husband and wife to treat each other as enemies. It is easy to look at your spouse and say they are to blame. They are the enemy. "He won't pull his weight." "She is always harping on me to do more around the house." "If he would do more I wouldn't feel so overwhelmed." "I don't like being at home because I feel attacked and there is always another project to do." Don't let this happen. It's impossible to build a great team if you think one of your teammates is the enemy. God, at times, allows big problems to come into our lives to change this "my spouse is the enemy" thinking. Finding the common enemy will significantly improve your marriage. The real enemies of life can bring couples together.

There is nothing as unifying as a common enemy. Sometimes the enemy is a relative who is relentless in their attack. Sometimes it's a friend who pulls one spouse toward evil plans. Sometimes an enemy is a job that is overworking a spouse. The enemies must be identified and fought together. It is the husband's job to help identify the common enemy so the family will band together to fight it. If the enemy is not identified, it usually results in couples seeing each other as the enemy. The husband or the wife cannot be the enemy.

## Identify the Natural Enemies of Your Wife, Marriage, and Family

There are certain natural enemies that come against a family. You or your wife may have a problem scheduling time, handling money, or saying no to outside activities or people. All these problems have an enemy behind them that needs to be identified and fought together.

In each of these cases, you or she may have a problem resisting the enemy, but by definition, she cannot be your enemy. Constantly ask the question, "What enemy is behind this problem?" It can't be your spouse.

Many times, your wife identifies you as the enemy, perhaps because you don't make enough money, spend enough time at home, get along with her side of the family, or maybe you drink too much at times. But you cannot be the enemy. You may be influenced by the real enemy but you are not the enemy either. Identifying the enemy correctly means husband and wife can fight the enemy together. Identifying the real enemy allows both husband and wife to see life from the same perspective. You can fight alcoholism together. You can fight low self-esteem together. You can fight past abuse together. You can fight a lack of financial wisdom together. You can fight an unhealthy generational pattern together. But you can't and shouldn't fight against one another. Neither of you is the enemy.

## Growth Exercises—What Are Some Problem Areas?

1. What are some problems that you and your wife disagree about?

2. What common enemies might be behind the above problems?

## Equip Your Wife and Family to Face the Common Enemy

After identifying the common enemy (an overbearing boss, screaming kids, video games, anger, drinking too much, food, outsized ego, technology/computer), you must equip yourself and your wife with funds, battle plans, and people to help. It is not enough to say, "You have to do better" or "go figure it out."

Realize that if your wife has an enemy, you have an enemy. You are to help her win her battles. If she battles her weight, you have to help her battle that enemy (even if you do not struggle in that area). If she has a battle with alcohol, you have a battle with alcohol. If you battle with anger, you both have an emotional enemy. If you are unwilling to marshal your resources to fight the enemy, your wife concludes, "I don't matter that much to him," or "He's not that interested in the marriage."

## Growth Exercises—What Are Some Common Enemies?

1. Identify some common enemies that might apply to you and your wife:

   - Lack of finances/financial stress
   - Anger, unrealistic expectations, violence
   - Nosy, intrusive relatives
   - Alcohol, drugs, porn
   - Immoral or bad influence friend
   - Church problems
   - Job demands and stress
   - A specific temptation to sin
   - Annoying neighbors
   - Unruly children or a problem with one of them
   - Lack of time/disorganization
   - Other: _____

2. Discuss a workable battle plan to conquer the common enemies you have identified. Realize that developing a plan will require lots of talks, lots of research, talking to experts, and help from people who know what they are doing. Your initial plan may not work, and you will have to make lots of plans before one works on the enemy that is destroying your spouse, your marriage, or your family.

3. What provisions are needed that you or your wife do not have now to work out your plan? This list will take energy to compile. Realize that there are things that will work if you and your spouse will perform them. Find these solutions, provisions, perspectives, and ideas.

4. What are some possible changes that can be made so that you and your wife may effectively battle the enemies in her life and your marriage?

## Do Battle against Pre-selected Enemies

In marriage and family, there need to be pre-selected enemies that the whole family can rally against together. Look for the activity, authority, or environment that is trying to damage your spouse and your children, and start fighting against it—together.

Some husbands have enrolled the whole family in a sport to battle the common enemy of inactivity and overeating. Some husbands have blocked all the TV channels because of negative influences coming from various programs. Some husbands have enrolled both husband and wife in a financial wisdom seminar so they can battle together against debt and impulsive spending. Some husbands have enrolled in counseling to battle the communication problem in the marriage. Some husbands have taken the family on a three-week vacation to battle the enemy of family independence and isolation. Some husbands have started a business with their spouses so that they could be together more. Some husbands have enrolled in al-anon to help battle alcoholism with their spouses. Be creative and look for the real enemy, not just the closest person to blame.

### Growth Exercises—Determine Pre-selected Enemies

Below are some of the pre-selected enemies that a husband can use to build unity in the marriage and family. Think through which ones could apply to you and your family. Are there any others? How will you rally your family to do battle against them?

| | | |
|---|---|---|
| Gangs | Racism | Ego |
| Homelessness | Gluttony | Environment |
| Finances | Drugs/Addiction | A specific disease |
| Poverty | Illiteracy | Evil music |
| Neighbors | Blindness | Unbelief |
| Pornography | Suicide | Profanity |
| Abortion | Laziness | Crime |
| Other: | Other: | Other: |

# 12.

## ENJOY SHARED EXPERIENCES

---

**M**ost women have the ability to visualize in a way men cannot. The ability to visualize allows them to enter into plans, images, and memories as though they are actually happening at that moment. This makes her more able to enjoy the wonder and power of memories. So the more special memories and shared experiences you can help her build in the corridors of her mind, the stronger the marriage.

In their work with couples who were in love, scientists found significant brain differences between men and women. Men in love had a lot of brain activity that integrated with the visual centers of the brain. Women in love, however, had much more activity in the areas that control memories. Men in love are significantly oriented by what a woman looks like, and women in love are much more oriented to the memories that they have with their loved ones.[5] How does a husband use this memory orientation to meet his wife's needs and increase her love for him? It would seem obvious…increase the positive memories that she has of you caring for her and for the family. I make a special effort to take pictures of all family outings, all work projects we do together, and all vacations so that my wife and my girls can see the fun we've had and remember the good times together.

During the rough times and dry periods of life, it is possible for your wife to go back and live in the good memories that she has experienced with you. These good memories sustain her and give her retreats and energy. If there is not a wealth of these good memories, she may begin to doubt that being with you is helping her.

She needs a steady and consistent number of positive times and loving expressions pouring into her life. If her only good memories of you and her are from a long time ago, then she will experience more low times. Each woman is different, but I encourage husbands to think of daily, weekly, monthly, and seasonal events that she can look forward to and look back on.

## Harness the Teachable Moments

A husband and father must be alert to those special moments when life lessons can be taught. When a man assumes this critical role of commenting on the teachable moments, those in the family can experience life in a much richer way.

Your wife needs you to point out the lessons and instructions that God is giving in the midst of a crisis. She needs you to have a cool head and see past the present difficulty. She needs you to say something like, "In a few years, we'll laugh about this!" "What do you think we will have grown from through this trial?" "I was reading in Scripture the other day… and I thought that God could be teaching us… because of this difficulty."

It is imperative that you do more than just responding to the crisis. You must rise above it. You may call for prayer. You may go to the Scriptures. You may point out what quality God is teaching. You may pull the most volatile person aside and speak to that person in soft tones with reassurance. You may put forth a battle plan on how to deal with the present situation. You may say something like, "Do you know what is so great about this?"

Whatever you do, you must transform the situation into a lesson and a potentially positive memory. Some groups call this having a parable perspective: always looking for a way to help life make sense. This is the type of man who blends his wife into his life by constantly filling her mind with memories of ordinary events that take on a whole new meaning.

## Growth Exercises—Harnessing Teachable Moments

1.  What are the ordinary events that could become teachable moments for you and your wife?

2.  Memorize the Beatitudes (Matthew 5:3–12) and the Fruit of the Spirit (Galatians 5:22,23), so you can be in touch with God's will when a crisis comes.

3.  Have a Parable Time this week. Let your wife and children point to different objects. Tell them how that illustrates an important lesson in life or a godly principle.

## Make Memories

The wise husband has plans and ideas that will fill his wife's mind with positive and loving memories. Most women have a corridor full of images in their minds. If your wife only has images of you screaming, then those are the images she will relive. The more positive the images, the more loving she will feel about the relationship. Here are some ideas to fill your life with positive memories:

*Take pictures of your dates and the exciting events that you and your wife experience together.*

This is easy these days with Instagram, Facebook, and camera phones. Hire a babysitter (if you have little ones) and take her to dinner and something fun, even if it is just a walk around the mall or to a movie. Dates can be delightfully fun, and if you think of a few questions ahead of time to ask her, you can explore her soul and yours.

*Create "memories" that have not happened yet.*

Every woman needs to have something to look forward to—something she is dreaming about and planning for. These future memories allow her to get through the tough times in the present. Typically, your wife needs three big things to look forward to per year. One in the Summer, one in the Fall, and one in the Spring. It should be something she likes to do, not just something she is dragged to because you enjoy it.

### Create a positive memory.

You can do this each night around the evening meal, cleaning up the dishes, playing a game, watching a program together, and doing homework. All of these are available for a positive comment, a joke, a discussion, a Scripture, or a prayer. Just focus on doing something positive, helpful, and fun each evening.

### Plan a little get-away or an extended date.

This can be for just the two of you or the whole family, whichever would be more delightful to both of you. Go see grandma, rent a hotel room in a nearby city, go see something you haven't seen in the region, go to a museum, take a tour, take a dessert tour at the food court or the downtown. Remember, she will go on this trip many times before it happens and after it happens because of her ability to visualize.

### During holidays, do something special that is associated with that time of year.

If you are not creative about this type of stuff, let your wife create a great time, and you get credit for being all for it. We did table game nights on New Year's, special get-a-ways on Valentine's day, new dresses and family dinner on Easter, Memorial Day at the lake, July 4th and fireworks, a Labor Day picnic or barbeque, Halloween treats, parties, and church events, Thanksgiving family gatherings, Christmas tree cutting and setting up, Christmas Eve Services, Christmas Day. You can insert so much positivity into your marriage and your family by being ready to embrace these positive moments. Don't be a drag on the event because you of something you would rather be doing. Be fully present and positive. Most often, the difference between a good time and boredom is whether you fully engage. It is your choice.

### Plan some kind of vacation so that you, your wife, and the whole family can do a lot of fun things.

This could be going to visit family and doing fun things when you are there. It could be something delightful like camping, amusement parks, church camps, or visiting new cities. There are so many ready-made ways to fill up your marriage if you will engage with your family. Be present, take a lot of pictures, make jokes, listen deeply, and ask questions of your spouse that go below the surface. Rejoice when difficulties happen because these will draw your marriage and family together.

Take lots of photos of all of these adventures. The ones at home, the ones each week, the ones each month, the ones each season, and the ones each year. I was always taking pictures, and everybody complained about them until they saw the pictures, and they all wanted the memory and the picture. My wife and my family have permanent pictures of all the fun and incredible things we did together.

## Growth Exercises—Memory Making

1. Ask your wife to tell you the dominant images about your marriage that she has in her mind. Ask her to tell you the most powerful pictures or memories she has of you. Are they good or bad?

2. Make a list of all the fun times that you and your wife have had together.

   - Start by saying, "Do you remember that time..."
   - Find the pictures of those happy times.
   - Go to a photo center and enlarge a picture of those good times.

3. Ask your wife for ideas about vacations, places to go, and special times she would like to do. Have her list out at least fifteen possibilities.

4. If you have a hard time thinking of fun things to do, ask other couples or individuals what they have done on vacations or special times. Someone will have something that sounds good to both of you.

# 13.

## PROTECT YOUR WIFE'S WEAKNESSES

A tragedy I see in marriage counseling is when husbands expose the weaknesses and flaws of their wives. This has become a favorite pastime of many men. It becomes almost like a game show: "How Stupid Is Your Wife?" "Dumb Things Women Do!" "Find the Flaw!" "I'll Bet My Wife Is More Foolish than Yours!" I can't even begin to tell you how misguided this is. It causes men to start looking for flaws instead of strengths, which is poison to the relationship.

This trend of exposing the weakness of our wives is destructive. Pointing out her weaknesses diminishes her reputation in the eyes of others. It diminishes our own respect for her. It focuses us on weakness instead of celebrating a strength. It removes her from the place of honor. Trust is destroyed if she hears about it.

Every one of us is broken. We all have weaknesses. There are things you don't do well either. Your marriage is supposed to be where your strengths are promoted and weaknesses are minimized. Why would a godly husband put his wife in a situation where her inability or lack of knowledge is exposed? It should never happen. This is what it means to "cherish" or protect your wife (Ephesians 5:28). A godly husband wants everyone to think that his wife has no weaknesses, only strengths. He consistently puts her in situations where her strengths shine through.

When I'm at work, I know the strengths of everyone on the team I'm leading. I assign the various tasks so that they will complete their tasks extremely well. Then I get to congratulate them on doing a great job. This is a positive feedback loop. I never give someone a task I know they will fail. If someone does fail at an assignment, I find out if it is a lack of training, a lack of ability, or a lack of desire. If it is a lack of ability, I do not offer training; I find a new assignment or role where they have the ability, so they can shine. Why would I not do the same thing for the most important person in my life, my wife? The most important team I am leading is my marriage and family. I must put my wife in roles where she will succeed.

One of the goals of marriage is to make the weaknesses of any team member irrelevant. The husband should take the lead in this focus-on-strengths approach. Because this is a partnership, what one person does not handle, the other often can handle well. What one partner does not understand, the other can step in and deal with. What neither partner does well should be hired out. Find a way to protect your wife from the things she does not do well.

Let me show you this through the example of four couples on the subject of budgeting. In one couple, the husband was good at big-picture budgeting but not the recording of transactions. His wife was good at transactions but not big-picture budgeting. So they found budgeting software where they could divide the budgeting job into these two areas. They both did what they were good at.

In another couple, the husband was good at budgeting, but the wife thought she was and didn't like her husband's budget restrictions. He let her handle the budget for six months, and it became a mess. She handed it back to him, realizing that the family was better with his restrictions.

The wife of another couple was really good at budgeting, but they kept arguing about how the money was being spent, and the heated discussions were not helping. They both asked a trusted friend who was great at budgets to handle their money, and she would handle the details. This has created harmony and a way to have nonangry input into how the money is spent.

In the final couple, neither one, husband or wife, wanted to handle the budget, so they kept shoving it on the other one. Both made a mess of it. They kept hating the process and saw their financial future get worse and worse. Eventually, they hated each other over their lack of financial progress. They harped on the weakness of each other so much that they divorced. They said it was over money, but really it was over a lack of imagination. The husband had an inability to protect his wife's weakness because he had the same weakness. They probably should have delegated the budgeting like the third couple.

There are all kinds of things that you or her may not do well. Do not focus on these. It is common for husbands or wives to...

not know how to clean well;

not know how a car works;

not budget effectively;

not host people at the home;

not know how a certain kind of business functions;

not know how to eat moderately;

not push away at shopping impulses;

not know how to decorate;

not put outfits together;

not discipline the kids effectively;

not homeschool;

and a thousand other things...

Find your wife's strengths and protect her weaknesses. There is always a way. Someone you know will have a workaround, a fix, a good solution. I am amazed at how God will guide you to an answer so that your wife does not have to look weak. I can remember one man who discovered that his wife could not cook at all during his honeymoon. She was a really horrible cook and almost set the house on fire when she tried the first time. He decided that he would do all the cooking for the family. He developed into quite a cook. I was at their house for dinner on several occasions and never suspected that this great family's wonderful wife and mother could not cook. I only discovered it years later in a very private conversation.

Men, you are not helping your marriage or standing at the office when you tell what your wife does poorly. It may produce a laugh at the moment, but it diminishes her and diminishes you as her protector. Step up and protect her reputation by only repeating the positives about her. This is what you are expecting her to do for you.

Marriage is fundamentally a team. When you become a team and protect one another, incredible things can happen: parenting works, finances increase, chaos turns into organization, children succeed, and so on. The goal of building unity in your marriage is to become a better team and accomplish more of your dreams. Be your own unique team.

### Growth Exercises—What Weaknesses Do You Need to Protect Her From?

1. Do you know what some of your wife's greatest fears are?
   Talk to her about them and list them.

2. What fears or struggles is your wife presently facing from which you cannot protect her? How will you support her through them?

3. What are your wife's greatest inabilities and areas of incompetency (cooking, sewing, organizing, mornings, sports, etc.)?
   (*WARNING: Do not write these down. Never record your estimate of her inabilities.*)

## Motivate, Encourage, and Protect Your Wife in Areas that Need the Greatest Improvement

Many men see that their wives could succeed by tackling a particular personal habit. These areas are often the topic of her husband's sarcasm and negative comments. This type of "change motivation" rarely works.

A husband who wants to see his wife improve will energize her to change through acceptance, not through pointing out her faults. Your wife will be energized to change when she sees you focus on her positive qualities. You rob your wife of the ability to change by harping on a difficult area. Just as you are not motivated to change if your wife nags about an area, she is resistant to being hounded into "improvement."

Remember that your job as the husbandman of the vine is to supply all she needs to grow and blossom to her fullest. She may "need" more affirmation, love, listening, or training, but she is not helped by yelling, criticizing, sarcasm, blaming, or shaming.

If there is an area where your wife really could grow, ask yourself how you can energize her so that she wants to tackle this issue. She needs to know that she has your unconditional support whether she tackles this area or not. If she knows that she is loved, then she may be able to grow in areas that are "impossible" for her to change. I have watched many wives who have gotten degrees, started a business, overcome fears, changed personal habits, and been open to new perspectives because they know that they are loved and accepted in the depth of their souls.

## Growth Exercises—How Can You Encourage Her to Grow?

1. What self-improvement projects is your wife working on this year? What are some positive ways you can encourage or help her achieve her goals? Write down 5–10. I have found that this is a good question to ask my wife when asked in a time of understanding and goal setting. Sometimes it needs to be preceded by the revelation of where you want to grow and develop this next year.

2. Here are some crucial things to remember when seeking to bring about change in anyone. Go over this list and check which ones you can do to incorporate this principle.

   - Build a legacy of appreciation and approval.

   - Ask what their dreams, desires, interests, and hopes are in each area of life.

   - Ask how they think they might achieve these goals in the various areas of life.

   - Ask how when the next time they encounter a situation or person, the outcome can be better or different.

   - Admit your errors before indicating something could have been better.

   - Ask questions to see if they understand the problem and a solution from a variety of perspectives.

   - Do not publicly shame or demand confession, repentance, or contrition.

   - Regularly praise for the slightest steps in a positive or helpful direction.

   - Paint a picture of the better, more noble person they can be.

   - Come alongside and inject courage, hope, perspective, and motivation.

   - Simplify the path over the obstacles: "It's easy. You can do it!"

   - Dwell on the rewards, benefits, and better future that will be gained by continuing to move in your direction.

   - Help your wife contemplate or understand what God might be seeking to develop in and through her.

# PRINCIPLE #5—AGREEMENT

"How shall two walk together unless they be agreed?"

Amos 3:3 KJV

⸺⸺

**They were splitting up.** Sally was leaving because Bruce was throwing her out. They could not talk about anything without it becoming a shouting match. When Sally decided to spend a large amount of money that Bruce was unaware of, he told her to leave home.

When I called this couple to talk about their marriage, they seemed unwilling to work on their relationship. He was totally beside himself. His wife would never let him talk about anything important without interrupting him. "We can't talk about anything!" he cried. "I end up just getting mad, and nothing gets decided."

"He's the one who never listens," she blurted. "He just makes arbitrary decisions without checking with me. If I have to live with his idiotic decisions and subject my kids to them, I would rather be on my own. Eventually, one of us just makes the decision that seems best, which he resents. We are not a marriage; we are two independent kings trying to coexist!"

Sadly, this situation occurs in many marriages, and it only worsens if the couple divorces and tries to handle custody arrangements through the courts. There is a better way to handle conflict than "I win/she loses" or "she wins/I lose" scenarios.

God reminds us through the prophet Amos, "How can two walk together unless they be agreed?" (Amos 3:3). It is not possible for unity unless there is consensus on decisions. If a husband is wise, he will involve his wife in almost all the decisions of his life, forever seeking her wisdom and the wisdom God communicates through her. I am amazed at the number of couples who don't have a system to work through areas where they initially disagree. This chapter will introduce a system that has worked for hundreds of marriages by allowing wisdom to reign in the marriage. Please keep an open mind before you reject these ideas, rather than thinking, "She will never go along with that" or "He just wants his way."

No one ever got married to fight with their spouse. We get married to love our spouse and be loved in return. But fighting and arguing are what many couples spend too much time doing. They don't have the necessary skills or tactics to create agreement, so they just live in conflict, but it doesn't have to be this way.

How can you move past conflict to wisdom? Aim at wisdom, not your own way. God is asking you to be willing to seek wisdom even though you probably have a personal preference. It's your job to help the two of you move away from conflict toward agreement. Don't worry, I'll show you how to master some basic skills designed for building agreement in a few moments. It involves moving from being childish in your thinking (self-focused) to being an adult (wisdom-focused). A husband really only becomes the head of the home when he is willing to dig for wisdom even though he already knows what he wants to do. You become a true husbandman and gardener of your family when you learn new things to make your family thrive. This takes work, but it is well worth it.

---

"For where jealousy and selfish ambition exist, there is disorder and every evil thing. But the wisdom from above is first pure, then peaceable, gentle, reasonable, full of mercy and good fruits, unwavering, without hypocrisy."

James 3:16,17 NASB

---

When I first wrote this chapter twenty-plus years ago, I only knew of a few skills for moving a couple towards agreement. Through studying the Scriptures, my marriage, and other couples I've counseled, these skills have proven to help couples stop all the fighting. I get comments from men all the time, "You don't know my wife." They're right, but I know that many husbands believe unity comes down to whether they married an agreeable wife. They think if she would automatically agree, the marriage would be great, but this isn't true. Many "agreeable" wives do not share their wisdom because they know they'll pay a heavy price if they do. They remain silent for fear of belittling, rejection, or retribution. I've personally witnessed men shutting their wives down through anger, disagreement, sulking, or walking away. But when they did those things, they missed out on new insights and knowledge she could have added to the situation, not to mention the emotional abuse those women felt. The better point of view is, "How do I draw out my wife's wisdom so our whole family can be blessed?"

Many of us have a path to action in our head that often moves us to say and do things before we have really heard the other person's point of view. One of the most helpful truths to get couples talking instead of fighting is to listen to the other person's point of view before launching into our own. Proverbs 18:13 (NASB) tells us, "One who gives an answer before he hears, it is foolishness and shame to him." This is so true.

In the book *Crucial Conversations*, author Kerry Patterson talks about communicating when the stakes are high, opinions vary, and emotions run strong. Patterson says that we all take a few bits of information, facts, or data into a conversation, and we prematurely draw totally wrong conclusions. These conclusions are built on a few facts and information but are filtered through our own perspectives and interpretations, causing us to become prisoners to them. We start to get emotional because of the conclusions and stories we tell ourselves, not because of the facts themselves. But unfortunately, we'll act on those emotions with anger through social media, email, texting, yelling in people's faces, etc.[6]

The following diagram on the next page illustrates this process happening to everyone, especially in today's day and age. Everyone has their information. Everyone has their conclusions. Everyone has their emotions. Everyone has their typical actions (talking, nagging, leaving, visible anger, and so forth). The husband's job is to direct the marriage towards wisdom and knowledge and away from emotion, anger, and conflict. Maybe there are other facts and information that need to be gathered. Maybe there is more than one conclusion or story to tell. Maybe different emotions will emerge. Maybe there are other actions and doings. But as the husbandman of the marriage and family, you have to realize that this process is happening to everyone, not just you. Your path to action may not be the wisest one. The addition of more facts, more conclusions, more emotions, and more potential actions will make you a wise leader instead of just a self-focused one.

# The Path to Action – ICED

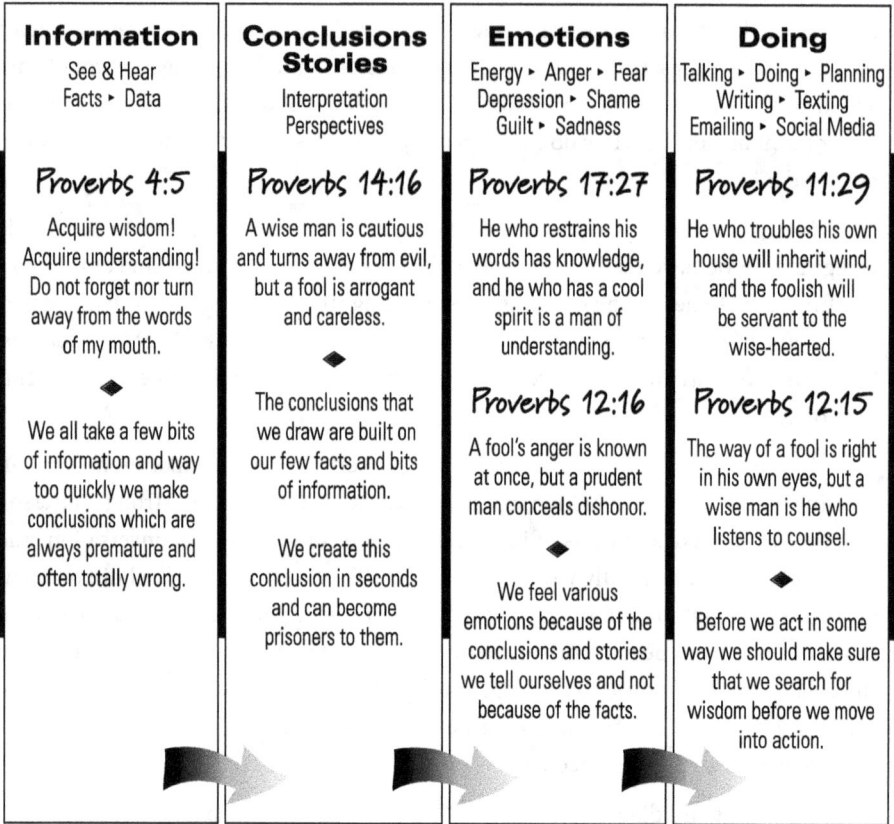

| Information | Conclusions Stories | Emotions | Doing |
|---|---|---|---|
| See & Hear Facts ▸ Data | Interpretation Perspectives | Energy ▸ Anger ▸ Fear Depression ▸ Shame Guilt ▸ Sadness | Talking ▸ Doing ▸ Planning Writing ▸ Texting Emailing ▸ Social Media |
| **Proverbs 4:5** | **Proverbs 14:16** | **Proverbs 17:27** | **Proverbs 11:29** |
| Acquire wisdom! Acquire understanding! Do not forget nor turn away from the words of my mouth. | A wise man is cautious and turns away from evil, but a fool is arrogant and careless. | He who restrains his words has knowledge, and he who has a cool spirit is a man of understanding. | He who troubles his own house will inherit wind, and the foolish will be servant to the wise-hearted. |
| ◆ | ◆ | **Proverbs 12:16** | **Proverbs 12:15** |
| We all take a few bits of information and way too quickly we make conclusions which are always premature and often totally wrong. | The conclusions that we draw are built on our few facts and bits of information.<br><br>We create this conclusion in seconds and can become prisoners to them. | A fool's anger is known at once, but a prudent man conceals dishonor.<br><br>◆<br><br>We feel various emotions because of the conclusions and stories we tell ourselves and not because of the facts. | The way of a fool is right in his own eyes, but a wise man is he who listens to counsel.<br><br>◆<br><br>Before we act in some way we should make sure that we search for wisdom before we move into action. |

Adapted from *Crucial Conversations*, Patterson et. all, 103-125, 2nd edition

## "He who is wise in his own eyes is worse than a fool"

In the next three chapters, I will show you how these skills can move your marriage toward harmony and greater wisdom. There are thirteen total, split up according to the chart below. You can learn to use these techniques at the appropriate times to change the nature of communication in your marriage. Agreement is achieved by knowing when to use these skills, which is either well before the conflict happens, the time when the disagreement is actually happening, or the period after the conflict.

I have found it helpful to carry a card with this chart or put it on your phone as a ready reference for what to do. You will be amazed at how well these principles work.

# Moving Beyond Conflict

| BEFORE (Chapter 14) | DURING (Chapter 15) | AFTER (Chapter 16) |
|---|---|---|
| Aquire Wisdom | Answer Gently | Apologize |
| Align Expectations | Abandon | Agreement System |
| Adapt | Ask Questions | Ask for Positive Changes |
| Appreciate | A.T.T.U.N.E | Action Plan |
| | Accept Influence | |

# 14.

## BEFORE CONFLICT SKILLS

---

### Acquire Wisdom

Gaining wisdom is one of the essential skills for softening a disagreement. Listen to the ancient wisdom of King Solomon, one of the most skilled conflict managers in the history of the world.

> Acquire wisdom! Acquire understanding!
> Do not forget nor turn away from the words of my mouth.
>
> Do not forsake her, and she will guard you;
> Love her, and she will watch over you.
>
> The beginning of wisdom is: Acquire wisdom;
> And with all your acquiring, get understanding.
>
> Prize her, and she will exalt you;
> She will honor you if you embrace her.
>
> She will place on your head a garland of grace;
> She will present you with a crown of beauty.
>
> Proverbs 4:5–9 NASB

---

We can start acquiring wisdom by first asking questions to understand why there is conflict in the first place. Everything was going along just fine, but now she's upset! You need to know what happened. Why is she upset? When there is a difference of opinion or a disagreement, this is your cue to go into wisdom-seeking mode rather than the crush-it or ignore-it modes. Don't try and reason with her—just try to find out where this point of view is coming from. Once she expresses her reason, you have a place to start.

In this section, I have added four pieces of practical wisdom to understand and remember about yourself and your spouse. These will be fun to discuss between the two of you. I've also added some growth exercises for you to do along with your wife. I hope you find them helpful.

*Become wise about your natural reaction to conflict.*

Conflict management experts have helpfully categorized typical conflict responses using animals so we can remember them more easily.[7] See if you can identify your wife's tendencies when it comes to conflict, as well as your own.

### Turtle: Hides from Conflict

This person tends to hide from conflict, hoping the matter will just go away. Just as a turtle pulls his head into his shell when danger appears, some people do this. A person with this kind of response has a tough time engaging in tense conversations and often just walks away or stays away if they think disagreement is coming.

### Shark: Attacks Conflict

The second type of response to conflict is attacking. The shark is always on the attack, always swimming forward. A person with this type of reaction to conflict has learned to do the same—attack. Whenever faced with a disagreement or a different point of view, this person's natural response is to question, ask for specifics, dispute, get louder, and disagree. Usually, the attack is verbal, but sometimes it can get emotional, even physical.

### Teddy Bear: Gives into Conflict

Giving in is another way some people respond when faced with conflict. We call these people Teddy Bears because they adapt to the environment they are placed in. When faced with a conflict of almost any kind, this person just gives up their idea or position and agrees with the other person.

### Fox: Compromises in Conflict

The fox is seen as a cunning animal capable of finding a way to win by giving as little as possible. A person who uses compromise to resolve conflicts is called the Fox because they want you to give in significantly, and they will only give a little bit. This usually becomes a negotiation if they have their way.

### Fire Ant: Everyone Loses in Conflict

The person who is willing to embrace personal loss if the other person also loses is called the Fire Ant. In nature, the fire ant will try and defeat an enemy, but if it is unable to, it latches on to the enemy and hurls both himself and the enemy to death. They will lose, but you will also lose.

### The Owl: Seeks Wisdom in Conflict

The owl is a creature who stands above the other creatures looking for the wisest solution. The person who is an Owl wants everybody to win and looks for the way that can happen.

I think it is safe to say that God would prefer we all become Owls, taking on the attitude where both people win, and God wins, too—the triple win (win/win/win). As we mature and grow in our faith, we can learn to react to conflict more wisely.

## Growth Exercises—What Is Your Natural Response to Conflict?

How do you and your wife respond to conflict? Pick from the list below what animal you each represent when it comes to reacting naturally in conflict.

|  | Husband | Wife |
|---|---|---|
| **Turtle:** Hides (avoidance) | | |
| **Shark:** Attacks (win/lose) | | |
| **Teddy Bear:** Gives in (lose/win) | | |
| **Fox:** Compromises (both win a little) | | |
| **Fire Ant:** Loses (lose/lose) | | |
| **Owl:** Wisdom (win/win) | | |

*Identify any destructive patterns.*

Next, understand any destructive patterns that show themselves in conflict. Many people have deeply embedded patterns, behaviors, tendencies, and unproductive reactions that lead them into damaging situations. I call these S.A.D. behaviors because so many of them start with "S," "A," or "D." These are things like sarcasm, accusations, or disrespect, which are immature ways of dealing with conflict because they keep the conflict going. Remember, our goal as the husband is to create a way of peace. We think our way is the best way to handle or recover from conflict, but as the scriptures say, our ways may be damaging or destructive.

————

"There is a way *which seems* right to a man,
But its end is the way of death."

Proverbs 14:12 NASB

————

"The wise woman builds her house,
But the foolish tears it down with her own hands."

Proverbs 14:1 NASB

————

Knowing how you or your partner is tempted to move in damaging or destructive ways is another step toward a peaceful solution. As the husband, don't let the negative patterns of the past damage your relationship. Instead, lead your wife to peace.

## Growth Exercises—What Are the Destructive Behaviors?

1. Look at the list of the S.A.D. behaviors below. Check all the behaviors that apply to you and what may apply to your spouse.

| S. | A. | D. |
|---|---|---|
| Silent Treatment | Anger | Dishonor |
| Sarcasm | Accusations/Blame | Demean |
| Slander | Attitude | Dismissive |
| Self-focused | Abuse: Verbal, Emotional, Physical, Sexual | Denial of Service |
| Spending | | Demands |
| Sick/Sleep | Avoidance | Dishonesty |
| Scheming | No Affection | Defensiveness |
| Stupidity | Addictive | Depression |
| Selfishness | Apathetic | Disrespect |
| Stubbornness/Irrational | Affairs/Adultery | Destructive Behavior |
| Unsympathetic | Unapologetic | |
| Spouse = Enemy | Abandonment | |

2. What are the embedded patterns you notice in you and your spouse? What types of actions, words, and reactions are invoked when conflict occurs? What happens because of conflict?

3. Discuss ways you can help each other move from the immature behavior toward the path that breaks down the conflict. As a couple, what can be your strategy for peace?

*Talk like adults.*[8]

There are three different perspectives, positions, or "voices" we can take when speaking to another person. First would be the "child voice," where we talk as a person who is not in control. Second, there is the "parent voice," where we talk as though we are in control and know what the other person should do. Third, there is the "adult voice," where we talk about different ideas and actions as an equal or peer.

In his fascinating book *The Science of Trust,* Dr. John Gottman tells us that in conflict, the *only* voice that works for resolution and harmony is the adult voice. Adults do not want to be talked down to, and they also do not resolve conflict when the other person is playing the victim. If we seek wisdom, we must talk using the adult voice, respecting all parties and valuing their contributions. This strategy works great on teens and young adults, too.

Here are some of the phrases that might be said in the adult voice:

"That is an interesting perspective."

"Let's add that to the possible solutions."

"In what ways could this be resolved?"

"I would like to recommend _____."

"I am comfortable (uncomfortable) with _____."

"What are the options that could be considered?"

"For me to be comfortable, I need the following things to occur ____."

If you or your spouse is used to speaking in the parent or child's voice, there must be an invitation out of that way of speaking and into an equal point of view. Yes, I realize some people just love the parent voice where they are dominant and tell everyone what they should be doing. But that does not lead to resolution and peace. And yes, I realize some people enjoy being the victim and hiding behind helplessness. But again, this "voice" does not lead to real resolution or peace.

When I got married, I can remember telling myself not to slip into a dominating voice, which had become so comfortable for me. Instead, I would invite my wife into an equal discussion of the facts and new perspectives. It was difficult at the beginning but has resulted in a wonderful marriage. I get to hear all of my wife's wisdom and add it to my own.

Dr. Gottman tells us that when we fail to use the adult voice, we significantly damage the marriage relationship and even our own health. "Having a self-interest-only perspective in a conflict conversation increased the husband's odds of dying...by over 11 times compared to a cooperative conflict conversation."[9] That is significant, don't you think?

*Look for the good, the wise, and the everybody-wins solution.*

Recognize there is knowledge, insight, development, a blessing, or an opportunity potentially hidden in every trial. The fact that a couple has conflict means there is room to grow. It could be a misunderstanding, a blind spot for one of the people, or a deep and ignored need in one person. It could also be an opportunity or a growth step for an individual or the couple. What is hidden in this conflict? James 1:2–4 (NASB) says, "Consider it all joy, my brethren, when you encounter various trials, knowing that the testing of your faith produces endurance. And let endurance have its perfect result, so that you may be perfect and complete, lacking in nothing."

In many cases, we don't often look for the benefit that will come out of a problem or quarrel; we just try to get past it and move on. But if we take the words of James to heart, we need this solution and its possibilities to discover something new. Realize that this new thing is there, but it must be discovered. So don't argue with your partner because she is the one who will help you find it. Work with her and keep your options open so you can find the good thing the conflict points out.

## Align Expectations

> "Make your ear attentive to wisdom,
> incline your heart to understanding."
>
> Proverbs 2:2 NASB

---

The second tool in building agreement is to align expectations before getting too far into the process. Several years ago, I was talking with a friend of mine, Jud Boise, a business consultant.[10] He uses a particular technique to increase success and productivity in companies, which he calls "aligning expectations," which he explains in his book, *Goals: Getting What You Want Most at Work and Home.* The exercise goes like this:

Jud asks the supervisor, "What are the five things you want your team members to be doing this week? Write them down and weight them in order of importance to you." Then he asks the employees, "What are the five things you think you should be doing? Write them down and weigh them in order of importance." Jud finds every time in a low-productivity environment that supervisors and team members have different lists in different orders. The supervisor talks with the employee about their two lists, writes down the five tasks or goals they have for the employee, and asks them to carry the card with him. When both supervisor and team members talk and align on priorities and expectations, the productivity jumps are tremendous. Just getting on the same page with this one simple question, "What do you think I ought to be doing this day or this week?" can change a company.

I have watched the same technique transform marriages. So many of the arguments couples have center around unmet expectations. "I thought we were going to the lake this weekend." "Well, I thought we would go to the zoo with the kids." Or, "I thought we would spend the tax money on fixing up the kitchen or the girls' room." "I thought it would go towards that new boat I have my mind set on." The couple knows a difference of opinion exists, but it's too much trouble to have a conversation ahead of time, so they have a fight when the difference shows up. Avoid the fight and ask your spouse what she is thinking about the weekend, the money, the activity, and so on. Discuss things before time to allow for differences of opinion and research for the wisest use of the time, money, energy, and people.

When my wife heard of this technique, she became ecstatic. She uses it all the time. She wants to know what I am thinking about all kinds of things, and this saves us so many difficulties. What are you thinking about the money we have coming in? How do you see this Saturday going? What do you think we can do for Jenessa's birthday? What do you think we could do for our date this Friday? This is good and keeps us talking, so we aren't surprised or disappointed by the future event.

Aligning expectations is critical to getting what you want and helps couples save so much frustration and pain. It means that both of you are willing to declare what you hope will happen and hear what the other person hopes will happen. It also means you are willing to think through ways to include the other person's ideas, adjust schedules and activities, or find a third alternative. The goal is to work together to create a win/win.

Too many couples keep quiet, hoping to sneak their plan into place without their partner noticing. It never works and will usually create hard feelings. There is always a way to make a win/win opportunity out of something that will be a win/lose situation if you don't talk beforehand about your expectations. I say to my wife all the time, "There are always options. I just need to know what you are thinking and expecting, and we can find something that will work for both of us."

Keep in mind that just because you or your spouse state the expectations, it doesn't mean that is what will happen. You are looking for wisdom, for the best thing.

It is possible that when your partner first states what they were expecting to do with the weekend, the vacation, the money, and so on, there could be a sense of doom or disappointment because it is so different from what you were expecting to do. They may feel the same way at first about your ideas, and that's okay. Just keep listening and be willing to talk about it. There is some unique way to do the best thing for everyone.

Some things you could say to her are:

"Let's work on aligning our expectations about this weekend, this pay-check, work week, date night... I want to make sure we are both on the same page."

"What do you see as the wisest use of this time, money, vacation, or weekend?" "What are we trying to accomplish? Is it realistic given our budget, length of time, energy level?"

"How much can we accomplish, and what are the most productive options to get the most done and have it be the wisest use of our time?"

"Do we want this vacation to be adventurous, relaxing, or both? What kind of activities do you want? Are there people we should try to visit?"

This process of aligning expectations is one of the great tools for marital harmony. It is so much better to avoid the fight with a straightforward conversation.

## Adapt

After acquiring wisdom and aligning expectations, move to the third technique for creating agreement and peace in your marriage, which is to adapt to her in some way. There may be some big or small adaptation you can make that will make all the difference.

---

"For this reason a man shall leave
his father and his mother,
and be joined to his wife;
and they shall become one flesh."

Genesis 2:24 NASB

---

"...and adapt to one another in the fear of Christ."

Ephesians 5:21 PHILLIPS

—

The Bible tells married couples to adapt or "fit in with" their spouse for a Christian union. They are no longer two individuals but one. What would it look like if you were to truly adapt or adjust to the woman you married?

Many men need to learn what their wife does each week and how she operates. Too often, we assume our wives are like our moms or that they enjoy all the tasks that have fallen to them. We wonder why things don't get done the way we think they should or why certain things get done but not others. To help resolve a conflict before it gets started, you need to adapt to her. Figure out what things she is good at and what she isn't, what she likes and doesn't like, then adapt, help, or bless her in some specific way.

What does adapting to your wife look like in real life? Think about adapting as more of an attitude of "What can I do to help?" Of putting her first, ahead of yourself. You know there are some things she will never be good at, so don't make her do them. She will always be interested in some things and not others, and if you adapt to reality, things will go more smoothly. If your wife doesn't like to camp, don't always suggest camping for vacation. If your wife enjoys shopping, then provide some money in the budget to go shopping. Talk to her about how her day went and what she liked and what she didn't. If she does not enjoy a particular type of movie, don't make those movies the ones you watch on date nights. Watch those by yourself. If she is not a great cook, but you are, you do the cooking. If a particular child is driving her nuts, step in more with that child. If she likes to talk in the mornings, find a way to talk with her in the mornings. If she has a skill in a particular area, help her find a way to express it. Help her achieve her goals and dreams where you can.

If you can learn to adapt to your wife, your marriage and wife will flourish, and you will have fewer conflicts and arguments.

## Appreciate

Learning to appreciate your wife is another crucial way to build unity and harmony. Keep acquiring wisdom, aligning expectations, looking for a way to adapt to your wife, and finding a way every day to be grateful and appreciative to her. When you have bathed your spouse in appreciation during the week, it is harder to have a huge fight. I recommend you thank your wife directly every time you notice something she did that was good. Even if what she did was expected or routine for her, appreciate her and let her know you saw it. Remember that so much of married life goes unnoticed and underappreciated. Notice the clean counters and be grateful. Notice the work she puts in at the office. Notice the great meal and thank her. Notice the groceries and tell her. Notice the hard work and write a note. Notice the sexual intimacy and thank her afterward. If you develop a habit of being grateful, it will change you and your marriage.

Look at what Scripture tells us in Ephesians 5:4 (NASB, emphasis mine), "And *there must be no* filthiness and silly talk, or coarse jesting, which are not fitting, but rather giving of thanks."

I stop each evening and write a note of appreciation to my wife for all the wonderful things I appreciate about her from that day. It could be things she has done. It could be things she is by nature. It could be ways she interacted with our children or with me. It could be about her work as a nurse practitioner. It could be about her work in our home. Doing this keeps me alert to all the positive elements in my wife's life. If I don't do this, I start taking her for granted.

You can start a perspective of gratitude in your home. Yes, you may have to go first for a while before she catches on, but it is worth it. Stop the next argument before it starts by being grateful for something about her every day.

# 15.

## DURING CONFLICT SKILLS

G abe always felt under attack whenever his wife, Darla, wanted to "talk." He would go into a defensive mode and couldn't hear anything she said. "I want to talk about last night," she would say, and immediately, he felt his tension and anger start to rise. He tried not to say anything, but he needed to let his frustration out. He'd end up pointing out something she had done or hadn't done to even out the conversation. Clearly, it didn't help. Before he knew it, he and Darla were furious, and nothing productive happened. They were at their wit's end.

Could Gabe learn a different series of responses to try during his next "discussion" with Darla when she started "attacking" him for something? Yes, of course, and it changed his marriage. Instead of seeing himself as "under attack," he changed his view of his role. He became the counselor or consultant to help his wife talk about her feelings and the problem she was having. She directed her frustration at him, but the issue was not necessarily about him. Once Gabe started using the skills presented in this chapter, their conflicts never went further than discussions, and they got along better than they ever had.

I want to suggest five techniques to try the next time a conflict or disagreement is underway. They defuse the tension and anger and bring the discussion towards a harmonious resolution. These are tried and true biblical solutions.

### Answer Gently

"A gentle answer turns away wrath,

but a harsh word stirs up anger."

Proverbs 15:1 NASB

———

When conflict ramps up, it's hard for men not to ramp up their emotions. The key is to stay calm and answer gently. If your wife is emotional and your desire is to match her emotional intensity level, *don't do it!* Lower your emotional and mental temperature and listen to what she says underneath her emotions. This is a crucial key to unlocking the door to harmony in your marriage.

I have watched huge muscular men become experts at defusing a marriage fight by just mastering this technique. When she is spitting and fuming, remain calm and ask her to tell you all about it. This allows your spouse to avoid escalating her emotion into a fight.

It is a natural reaction to want to defend yourself against a powerful onslaught of emotions. You want to fire back with an equal level of emotion. I get it. But don't be sucked into that trap. It will only result in a full-blown fight, and nothing will be accomplished except damage to your marriage. If your wife is full of emotion, let her get it out. Don't match her emotion as a defense against what you are saying; instead, talk to her gently and with empathy to draw out her emotion. Yes, she wants change, and she wants it now, but now is a time for talking and listening. Think of it as taking on the role of counselor and consultant. Don't get drawn into defending yourself; just listen. Don't get tempted to remind her about how she has messed up in the past; just listen. Don't overpower her emotion with your emotions to make her stop; just listen.

When she or you have very strong emotions that have not been expressed, it is like you are emotionally constipated. You will not feel normal until you get all that backlog of feeling out. It needs to come out, and there will be no reasoning until it is out. This is why science tells us we need to tell someone about our feelings before we can begin feeling normal.

Dana and I have a rule in our house that whoever got started first with an emotional discussion or has the stronger emotions gets the floor, and together we will explore their point of view thoroughly. We will come back to the other person's perspectives and emotions later if needed. This one-emotional-outburst-at-a-time rule allows the other person to remain calm and listen. Gentlemen, the great danger is that if you shut down your wife from telling you what is bothering her, you keep your marriage from growing to an intimate place. If she cannot tell you about her feelings, you will be stuck in a low intimacy-business relationship. Realize her emotions are doorways into her soul. She needs you to be calm as she tells you all about her concerns, irritations, anger, and difficulties with the various people and situations in her life, including you. Remain calm and listen; ask her questions about what she is saying. There is nothing to solve or fix during the conversation. *The conversation is the fix.* If changes are needed, you can talk about those after the emotional time has passed.

## Growth Exercises—How Can You Gently Say, "Tell Me About That?"

- Change the tone
- Change the body language
- Change the facial expression

## Abandon the Quarrel, Emotions, and Self-focused Perspective

> "The beginning of strife is like letting out water,
> so abandon the quarrel before it breaks out."
>
> Proverbs 17:14 NASB

We have already talked about the absolute need to answer gently. It would help if you now abandoned your emotions and any self-focused reaction to what she is saying. To become masters at defusing emotional situations, we must be able to abandon our normal emotional responses. This means we abandon the arguments we could say, the self-focused perspective that is naturally within us. Instead, we need to be open to learning something new. I can practically see you rolling your eyes, thinking, "I can't do this!" I'm here to tell you that you can! We've done it before at one time or another. For example, have you ever been in the midst of an argument or a heated conversation, and the phone rings? If it's a significant person on the line and we need to take it, we will immediately change our tone and our words in a split second to talk to this other person. When we do, we have abandoned our emotions and our argumentative stance to take that call!

The skill of abandoning (in this conflict-sense only) is super helpful in bringing harmony back to the forefront. You will feel yourself wanting to say things, but you won't. You will feel your emotions rising inside you, but you will keep them from taking over. You will hear all kinds of arguments (in your head) that would put her down or allow you to win, but you will not say them. Instead, you will draw her out and listen intensely to her emotions and perspective.

Proverbs 17:14 (NASB) tells us: "The beginning of strife is like the letting out of water, So abandon the quarrel before it begins." This scripture tells us to let all the emotion and the arguments go and seek harmony instead. This is the wise way to handle conflict. Proverbs 20:3 (NASB) says, "Keeping away from strife is an honor for a man, But any fool will quarrel." The self-focused person has to quarrel and make their point. But as you grow as a person, you realize that you win more by creating harmony than by winning a particular argument.

Sometimes, you will feel a rush of emotion or thoughts, but please, don't go with them. Listen, remain calm, and let the emotion go. This takes practice. You may not be able to hold back your feelings or arguments every time. When you are about to say things you know you shouldn't say, realize you are being flooded and excuse yourself. Tell your spouse or whoever, "I'm sorry, but I cannot have this discussion right now." Leave the scene. Keep quiet and get ready to listen. It would be better to say nothing than what will wound and hurt.

We have a rule in our home that if one of us is overwhelmed with emotions or can't keep from saying all the things we are thinking, we take *two hours or two days* to calm down before talking about it. The amount of time depends on how long it takes one of us to abandon the emotions and be able to carry on a calm conversation. This is a self-calming technique that can save your marriage. I am often called in after a couple has dropped verbal nuclear bombs on each other. They were trying to win an argument, but they killed a marriage. It doesn't have to be this way. Abandon the quarrel, abandon the emotions, abandon the self-focused perspective.

### Growth Exercises—What are Some Ways to Self-calm During a Conflict?

1. What always gets you overly emotional?
2. Think of those things and don't respond.
3. Become practiced at being emotional without letting it take over.

## Ask Questions

"The mind of the discerning acquires knowledge,
and the ear of the wise seeks knowledge."

Proverbs 18:15 NASB

---

It is time to move on to the third technique when the conflict is happening. We have looked at answering gently, abandoning the emotions and the self-focused perspective, and now we ask questions to learn what your spouse is really saying. In the middle of a conflict, one temptation is to make a negative statement or ask negative questions designed to win the argument or embarrass the other person. But I encourage you to ask information-gathering questions only. Your wife will usually wrap her point, her truths, in an emotional container because that is how she is experiencing it. She is frustrated or fearful or angry or sad, or lonely. Your job is to unwrap the emotion and find the real issue. Sometimes the issue is the emotion itself, but most likely, it is some idea, problem, future possibility, person, or concern. The better you become at asking questions, the quicker she will calm down.

Each time your wife wants to discuss a problem, think of it as a thirty-minute to one-hour-long puzzle. Don't get sucked into arguing. Embrace the fascinating adventure of learning all about what she wants to say. Asking lots of questions is how you'll sort out the pieces and find what the puzzle will reveal. Don't assume you know what it's all about. She should tell you even if you think you already know. By asking questions, you allow her to explore all sides and feelings of the problem, to put into words what she's trying to express. Ask every kind of question you can. This is what a good girlfriend would do. In fact, she hopes for that ... "Oh, tell me all about that!" The best way to defuse a problem is to explore it—not ignore it or get angry.

When you are in the middle of a discussion that has the potential to become heated, tell yourself, "What are all the questions I can ask her, so I understand her perspective better?" Ask every who, what, where, why, when, and how question you can think of. Gently asking questions defuses the negative emotion and tells your wife you love her. Plus, good questions unearth possible solutions to the issue. Remember, though, you are not looking for a solution at this point, only for understanding. If you rush to a solution (even the right one) too quickly, your wife may suspect you are not really willing to listen to the whole story. If she's ever told you, "You're never there for me," or "You just don't listen," this is why. She wants you to listen to the whole story to see where she's coming from.

In *The Science of Trust*, Dr. Gottman also tells us that 70 percent of marriage problems will never be resolved. One likes mornings, and one likes late-night. One is tidy, and one is messy. One is loud, the other quiet. One thinks that play comes only after the work is done, and one thinks you should always be ready for a little fun. One is very frugal, and one is much more free-spending. All of these and thousands of other issues could be problems your marriage faces. But happy couples learn to laugh about these "unresolvable" differences.[11]

The good news is that each problem does not have to be resolved in a marriage. The goal is harmony and joy, not "we have to agree on everything in all cases." Even if you have just had a huge fight or discussion and everyone agrees that something will be done a certain way, it may not change all that much because the other person was convinced against their will. The happiest couples embrace and accept who their partners really are and love them with all their quirks and idiosyncrasies. This does not mean you should embrace immorality, addiction, or illegality, but you should find a way to be loving, peaceful, and harmonious. How can a joyful family emerge from the blending of the two of you? You, husband, will have to do a lot of listening, asking, and adapting, and so will she.

## Attention

> "You husbands in the same way, live with your wives in an understanding
> way, as with someone weaker, since she is a woman;
> and show her honor as a fellow heir of the grace of life,
> so that your prayers will not be hindered."
>
> 1 Peter 3:7 NASB

Dr. John Gottman and his team use a simple six-step strategy to help couples tune in to each other through undivided attention.[12] I have found it to be quite effective in my own practice whenever I'm helping couples resolve conflict. When you are in the middle of a disagreement or discussion where emotions may boil over, these little tricks can help the conversation stay a discussion rather than turning into a huge fight.

*Step 1: Pay your undivided attention to your spouse.*

Put 100 percent of your focus on your spouse. Don't read the paper, keep the TV on, or check your phone.

*Step 2: Face them to let them know you are focused.*

Face your spouse, so they are looking at you, and you are looking at them. Something powerful takes place when a couple is calm and looking at each other. The temptation is to look away because the tension is high.

*Step 3: Let them talk and say it all.*

Don't shut down because what they are saying is emotional, wrong, or difficult. If you are going to grow in your harmony, you have to hear what they want to say.

*Step 4: Stay curious about what they are saying and feeling.*

Your spouse has emotions about things you don't get emotional about, and you need to know she is sensitive or reactive to things differently than you. Realize that if you are going to have a great marriage, you will need to understand their reactions (emotions), actions, and thoughts. The whole package of this person drew you in the first place, so the more you understand them, the more attraction you will usually find.

*Step 5: Stay open and don't become defensive.*

Develop the ability to listen without immediately rejecting what is said or becoming defensive to put off the other person. Just because you think you are not being defensive doesn't mean you aren't. Your spouse needs to feel you can listen with non-defensiveness.

*Step 6: Consider their feelings and thoughts to be valid.*

Empathy is called for in every relationship, especially in marriage. You want to connect with your spouse by feeling what they feel. You may not stay in that emotional place for long, but it is essential you embrace their space emotionally. A helpful word picture is when the wind is blowing, each stalk of wheat needs to bend under that wind to the same level. If one of the stalks resists and refuses to bend, it breaks under pressure. It shows you don't really understand, and the relationship is damaged.

## Accept Influence

"Through overconfidence comes nothing but strife,
but wisdom is with those who receive counsel."
Proverbs 13:10 NASB

Another insight from Dr. John Gottman and his team is that couples who have happy and successful marriages are those who readily accept the influence of their spouse. There is none of the "it is coming from you, so I suspect it or reject it" attitudes. Gottman suggests there are negative impulses you want to avoid: *disengagement* from the ideas, emotions, and communication of the spouse and *overreaction* to the ideas, emotions, and communication of the spouse. These negative reactions will cause your spouse to eventually pull away and emotionally disengage from you and the marriage. You may think you have won the argument, but really you have lost your wife.[13]

I see this disconnect in many husbands who come to me for help. They want a better marriage because there is so much tension and rancor in the house. Many don't realize that their years of disengagement (walking away, no response, changing the subject, turning on the television, checking their phone) or overreacting (anger, accusations, blaming, yelling) caused the environment they now live in. They have made their bed and must lie in it.

*The way forward to a good marriage is to listen to your wife's ideas and emotions.*

Reading that sentence may be overwhelming to you, but it is the way forward. Your wife is an intelligent person with perspectives, ideas, and feelings. Your job is to listen to her, understand her, and build a life with this woman. You can't wipe out who she is and expect to have a great marriage. This does not mean you will have to do things her way. But it does mean you must be open to hearing her way and her feelings.

The wise person is willing to listen to wisdom wherever it comes from... even an enemy, even from your spouse, even in this book. Look at what the proverbs say about being willing to listen and receive counsel.

---

"Listen to counsel and accept discipline,
that you may be wise the rest of your days."

Proverbs 19:20

---

"Strike a scoffer and the naive become shrewd, but reprove one
who has understanding and he will gain knowledge."

Proverbs 19:25

---

Husbands who make the most significant turnaround in their marriage embrace the personhood of their wife. They begin listening every day to their wives and what they have to say. Yes, your wife can be wrong. Yes, she can be misguided from time to time, and so can you. The team of both of you will help you as individuals be the best you can be. What is your wife actually saying? What is your wife feeling? What would your wife like to do? What is your wife thinking about the problems and situations in your marriage? If she can sense you are truly listening and willing to consider her point of view, fears, and potential solutions, you have a chance at a godly marriage. It is on you to husband your wife in the midst of conflict by being willing to accept her influence on you.

Let me also say that there are times when I run into men who have never voiced their opinions, feelings, or even their own dreams for the whole of the marriage. This also can cause a marriage to stay stuck on one channel and not move to the heights of intimacy. If this sounds like you, I would suggest talking with a counselor or a pastor about developing a strategy for getting your ideas out into the marriage. I usually find this a problem with wives hiding their ideas, feelings, or dreams, but it can also be a problem for some men. Typically, the most dominant personality must work hard at pulling the adaptive person's opinions, ideas, and dreams into their marriage.

## Growth Exercises—How Can You Draw Out Her Ideas?

1. Ask your wife for her ideas on something.

2. Ask your wife what her dreams are for five years in the future.

3. Ask your wife her opinion of something happening in your city, state, or country.

4. Ask your wife what she is feeling today.

# 16.

# AFTER CONFLICT SKILLS

Once you've had that disagreement, what can you do to restore harmony? Four techniques can help you profit from conflict. First, we'll look at the elements of a good apology. Then we'll look at an effective agreement system if the conflict has not been totally resolved yet. We'll learn how to ask for the positive changes you want, not the negative actions you don't want, and how to create an action plan for how to move forward as a couple on the issues you disagree about. Let's take a further look at each of these.

## Apologize

If you had a discussion or an argument with your wife and you know there were some things you did wrong or things you failed to do, then an apology is in order. For many men, apologizing is one of the most complicated things to get right. We tend to add certain phrases and ideas into our apologies, rendering them useless. We say things like, "If I did anything wrong," "You are also wrong," "It was not my intention," "If you think I did something wrong," "I said I'm sorry, can't we get past this?" "I'm sorry, but...." None of these sayings work because they are you-focused, not her-focused.

A good apology allows enough time to get to the heart of the matter. This pattern for a good apology will significantly change the conflict dynamics between you and your wife.

### Gentle in Approach

Start with a gentle approach. Use a soft and gentle tone (in many cases, it is best to almost whisper).

### Explore What Is Wrong

Tell your wife that you know what you did, or failed to do, hurt her. Ask if she could educate you about how your actions or inactions wounded or hurt her. This approach goes back to seeking wisdom and listening so you will truly understand the issue at hand. By seeking a rebuke here, you are becoming a wise man.

### Admit What Is Wrong

Once you allow her to explain what she saw as wrong, you can say, "I realize what I did was wrong." If the disagreement happened because of a misunderstanding, you can suggest it could be a misunderstanding. Be careful, though. I have often found that many men want it to be a misunderstanding rather than their being wrong. Usually, the wife still believes the husband is wrong in nine out of ten cases. This means the husband should assume he is wrong and it is not a misunderstanding.

### Seek Forgiveness

After admitting you are wrong, ask for forgiveness. Say, "Will you forgive me?" and wait for a "yes" or a "no." She needs to say, "Yes, I forgive you." If she is hesitant to say she forgives you, go back and explore the hurt some more. She may need to talk about it a little more before she can let it go. Allow her to do so—it will be worth it.

### Develop a Repentance Plan

If the hurt is very serious or one you have done several times, you may need to develop a repentance plan to prove you are taking the matter seriously. A repentance plan shows her and yourself that you do not want to do this offense again because it is causing problems in the marriage. Sometimes, the repentance plan is something she gets to do to you if you do it again. Other times, it is an action you have to do if you do it again. It could also be an accountability agreement with another person.

### Test for Openness

Finally, test for openness. Try changing the subject or hug her to see if she is open toward you. If she doesn't want to talk at all or is closed to a hug, there may be something unresolved in the issue. I have found that a deeper issue hides under a surface issue in some cases. There is no real healing of the marriage until the deeper issue is talked about and dealt with. If this is the case, go back to step two and see if there is more to this topic, situation, or difficulty.

## Growth Exercises—How Do You Know If You Should Apologize?

- Apologize for something you failed to do.
- Apologize for something you did.
- Apologize for something you have repeatedly done that offends her.

## Agreement System

Many disagreements in marriage come about because one spouse unilaterally makes decisions or makes them too quickly without including the spouse. I worked with a husband who consistently made impulsive decisions because they sounded right to him. He would rush off and decide to spend money or hire this person or set his sights on a particular goal, all without giving the decision enough time or asking his wife what she thought about it. When he finally slowed the process down and began incorporating her input, better decisions and actions increased in his life.

In another example, I was coaching a husband on how to save his marriage. He and his wife had had a serious disagreement on a matter about raising the kids. He disagreed with her and she left the house and went to stay with a friend. His wife has very strong opinions and believed that her solutions should be followed. He disagreed with her ideas and thought that some of them were too harsh. I advised him to create a decision chamber, which is the five-fold decision-making process we'll delve into down below. The decision chamber is where her ideas, his ideas, and other ideas are deposited and sorted through over some time. Only the wise ones would be let out—those decisions both spouses could wholeheartedly agree on implementing. He repaired the relationship by working with his wife to find a much wiser solution than her initial idea and his initial idea.

God gave you a wise woman who sees life from a different perspective. When God cannot get through to us, He will nudge our wives to oppose a decision until we listen to Him. We must realize that God has blessed us with a woman who is an equal heir of the grace of life (1 Peter 3:7). If our decisions are tempered with our wives' love and wisdom, our decisions will be better. Remember, God is not holding you responsible personally for making every decision; He is holding you responsible for the decision made.

One of the key ideas I have communicated to husbands is that since they are married, they cannot simply do what they think is best. In the past, before you were married, you got to make whatever decision seemed best to you and for you. But as a husband, you have a wife and maybe even a family to consider. God is commissioning you as the husbandman of the garden to make sure the wisest decision is made. How foolish would it be for the gardener to make decisions he liked without considering how the vines and the grapes would respond. What is the wisest decision? It's the best for everyone—a Triple-Win decision: God wins, your spouse wins, and you win. You can't make a decision that only benefits you. Your wife, children, and the people around you are waiting for you to move from a self-focused place to an others-focused place called wisdom.

This is a training process for both of you. Your wife, too, will have to make many decisions in your marriage that will affect your life and family in large and small ways. If either of you makes a series of selfish decisions, you could seriously damage your marriage and future. If you are both invested in this process of a wise decision, everything will go so much better. When you move from impulsive, self-focused choices, she can also. When you incorporate her insights, ideas, and perspectives, she can also incorporate your insights, ideas, and perspectives.

Commit together to make no significant decisions without agreement. Make a covenant to work as a team. Yes, this requires a lot more talking and listening than you have done in the past. Yes, the first discussion about any pending decision may be full of inaccurate statements, emotions, personal preferences, family of origin issues, and the like, but you are implementing a process that moves beyond one discussion and pushes for wisdom. If one of you is at the store and notices a bargain on a bigger-ticket item, but it's not something you've discussed, you either call and talk it over or walk away from a great deal. Both parties must feel that the other person will not sabotage the "team" for personal desires or gain for this to work.

### The Decision Chamber: Coming to Agreement

A good decision does not just happen. It moves through a series of fairly predictable steps and stages. Many men and couples try to shortcut these phases to arrive at a quick decision. Slow down the process and allow wisdom to be the goal, not your way. Examine your ideas, her ideas, and ideas from other trustworthy sources, like counselors, pastors, other adults you know, and resources on the subject. The system I propose is flexible and allows a couple to walk through the major points of making a good decision. These five phases are in order, but some can be done almost simultaneously.

### *Phase 1—Discuss the Issue*

It is very important to have an open discussion where opinions and questions are shared at the beginning of any decision-making process. Many spouses feel that decisions are being rammed down their throats because they never got to share their opinions on a proposed change. This is true at work, church, and home. The husband guides the discussion by saying, "This is just a discussion; it is not what we will decide." "Here's what I am thinking at this moment." This way, your wife can enter the discussion without worrying about an action she's not comfortable with following the discussion. I find it best to present the issue first rather than your solution. Here's what that might look like:

> "I wonder what you think we should do with the tax refund check. I have some ideas, but I want us to find the wisest thing to do with it."

> "I would like to talk about how to make your family's visit to our house more enjoyable for them and our family."

> "I see a potential problem with our schedules when the summer hits and the kids are out of school. I wonder if we could think through all the possible solutions to the problem."

> "Our budget will not work over the long-term, and we need to either make more or spend less. I want to discuss how we could do these things."

> "I would like to talk about the party we had last weekend. What went right, and what could be improved?"

Whoever brings up the topic should come having clear ideas about this topic. It is helpful to share your thoughts and perspective with flexibility. Make it clear that these are just opinions that you have right now about this topic. State your willingness to be informed, redirected, and influenced in a new direction.

People will see any topic differently, such as the consequences of an action. While one person may be looking at all the positives that will come from a particular course of action, another may be accurately assessing all the negatives. We need to see as much as possible about a decision before making it.

Part of discussing is listening, so it is important to let the other person discuss and share openly and freely about your topic without interrupting. It is helpful to take notes on what your spouse is saying. You are not trying to refute what they are saying but understand their perspective. If there is no true listening, the other person may react emotionally. Be open to allowing the other person to explore without shutting them down. There has to be a way of de-emotionalizing the discussion. Both parties need to share their perspectives on the issue over the course of the discussion but not as a rebuttal to each other.

### Phase 2 —Explore Options

At some point in discussing a topic or problem, people begin to share their potential solutions. These solutions or perspectives usually could be ranked in order of acceptability. When these acceptable options are ranked, the basic elements of that person's perspectives and needs emerge. It is important to realize that people include what they think is essential in their options. Look for these essential ingredients.

God wants you to make a wise decision so your marriage can flourish for both individuals and your family. There are answers out there to every dilemma you will face. Most unwise decisions take place because of a lack of possibilities or limited imagination. "Our family has always done this and I want to do that also!" is a really bad way of making decisions.

It is incredible how many new options and possibilities appear when you allow for open discussion and freedom to explore. I often have couples come back and report how smart their spouse is or how amazing things worked out over and above what they could have imagined.

### Phase 3—Seek Counsel

A good decision is made with the counsel of others outside the home. For the possible solutions, each spouse needs to engage in a series of conversations with experts, online searches, research from experts, or discussions with trusted friends or family members. Their insights, facts, and new options will help determine where everybody wins.

I always instruct couples to ask each other: "Who do you want me to check with to get a broader perspective?" The goal is to get more good ideas and new perspectives about the issue. Discussing where to seek counsel eliminates two key problems:

1.  You avoid checking with people who are not wise (husband's beer buddies or wife's coffee klatch). I have seen many marriages strained to the breaking point because the wife knows that the only people advising her husband are unsuccessful and unwise. When your wife does not have confidence in the people you are checking with, she cannot have confidence in the decision. Conversely, suppose you believe that every idea you have to improve the family will be discussed with ladies you do not respect. In that

case, you may resist discussing your potential decisions with your wife and begin making them unilaterally.

2.  You avoid overlooking counselors who would be helpful (wishing you would ask the pastor about this idea, hoping you would check with a financial planner, wishing she would talk to her dad about this, etc.). While it is hard to ask people for help and counsel, it is essential to do so. We often feel out of place as adults if we ask people we respect for help or counsel. This, however, is a part of making a good decision, especially on more significant issues.

## Phase 4—Commit to Prayer

This phase is where you pray together and ask God to guide you to the wisest decision. Lay out all of the possible solutions in front of God and ask Him to convince both of you of the wisest decision. Both husbands and wives must embrace the idea that God can and will work to help them see wisdom if they ask for it. Prayer is important for several reasons:

God can shape your desires and will during prayer time.

God can miraculously remove the problem in a way you would not have thought of.

When a couple prays, they come together in a unique way. It creates unity.

It is also important for a wife to see her husband leading her and the family to God for decisions and direction.

It produces trust and loyalty as problems start working out well.

Praying together by taking turns brings various aspects of this problem or situation to God. Let each person freely talk with God from their unique perspective on the issue. You may want to pray from many angles about this situation. It is helpful to pray in short sections and not let one person pray for an extended time.

After praying about a decision or direction, reflect on what God is saying. Does a scripture verse come to mind? Does a specific direction no longer seem ethical? Are you aware of people who would be wounded or hurt by this course of action? Is there a new awareness of God's positive direction in a particular way? It is helpful to talk about these.

Let me give you a very real example. My wife and I pray together before we go to bed every night, and we may use the time to pray about a pending decision. We also have an ottoman in our living room that we call the prayer ottoman. She or I will suggest that we pray around the ottoman when something is bothering us or think the whole family needs to pray about something. When we are in the prayer phase of a decision, I will say, "I think we need to take this decision about the vacation or how to spend the tax money to prayer." Everyone in the family knows that this means we will all kneel around the ottoman and pray individually about the decision we are contemplating. We will ask for wisdom. We will ask for clarity about what is not the right decision. We will ask for new facts, new direction, and new conversations. We do not assume we know the right answer but genuinely ask for guidance to find the right one.

### Phase Five—Making the Decision

There will come a point when a decision is obvious or needed. This is when the final discussion begins. It is important to remember that as the husbandman of the marriage and family, you are not given the authority to make the decision you want, but you are given the responsibility to ratify the best decision for the marriage and family.

Because the various options will have been discussed multiple times and all consequences considered, one path or decision usually begins to stand out. When it is clear that the majority of the facts, experts, consequences, and even feelings point to a particular decision, start the final discussion with your spouse. This cannot be the imposition of your original idea; it should be the open acknowledgment of what is the wisest decision in this instance. You and your wife should be past remembering who said what at the beginning. You are looking for what is best for your family.

First, clarify carefully the decision you are heading towards. *Also, make it clear that now is the time for this decision to be made.* I have seen marital troubles erupt because it was not clear that the decision was being made at that moment.

*"At this point, I am leaning in this direction as to what is best for our family..."*

There are other ways to begin the final discussion, "Honey, it seems clear to me that we need to go in this direction about the house;" "I think it is decision time on the kids' school situation." In some way, your wife needs to know that you are taking a final step.

Next, allow her to share anything you do not know or have not considered with you.

*"Has any new information come to light?"*

Your wife may have learned about something never considered before, or new information will come out. Before a decision is made, this information needs to be brought out to avoid going back on your decision. Give your spouse the chance to bring new information to the discussion even at this late stage. It is okay to learn, change, or reconsider right before a big decision. Most good decisions are double-checked right before they become permanent.

Then, allow discussion on any new consequences or if some new result has emerged.

*"Have any new options, ideas, or consequences come to light?"*

For example, "I talked to Sally about our desire to move into that community. She said that she had a friend do it, and the neighbors completely shunned them because they didn't drive the right cars. Their children were not even allowed to play in the other kids' houses." Things like this and a number of different circumstances and consequences would be good to know before a final decision is made.

When you make a final decision, it is usually obvious what the best course of action is, but it is always helpful to say your reasons for making the decision you made.

*"It seems that the decision needs to be _____ for the following reasons..."*

As the husband, you are not given authority to make your decisions, but you are responsible for making wise decisions for your wife and family. The more differently you and your wife feel about a subject, the more formally you need to follow this process. The more similar you and your wife are, the more informal and quickly these phases can go by.

I can remember sitting in the living room of Rob and Laura's house, trying to help while they were yelling at one another at full volume. After listening to this roar for a while, I realized they had no idea how to make a wise decision. They were so upset that they just impulsively decided things and readied themselves for the yelling match that would inevitably come later. I always thought couples knew how to come to a good decision. However, at this couple's house that one night, decades ago, I realized they didn't have a clue that there was a process for making good decisions together. I interrupted them and asked if I could teach them a different way of living, explaining that this selfish decision-making process led to fighting and would lead to divorce if they didn't fix it.

They agreed, and I explained this process to them. It clicked for Rob, but not so much for Laura. He began leading his family toward wise decisions, and some really good things started happening in their marriage and family. However, Laura decided after six months that she did not like having her selfish decisions eliminated through discussion and counsel. She was unteachable and wanted her own way. She used her crying, silence, and sexual favors as ways to get what she wanted, but those tactics weren't working anymore. She'd had enough and divorced him.

This is not the typical response for most wives. But all of us can decide to be selfish. Usually, the husband decides it is too much trouble to talk this much and be given new information that contradicts his previous opinion. Many husbands drop out of trying to be a godly husband at this point because wisdom must be searched for, and it is hard work at times (Proverbs 2:2–7). I am happy to say that even after the deep pain of divorce, Rob continued to grow as a godly husband and eventually went on to a wonderful, grace-filled second marriage to a lovely Christian woman built on wise, mutual decisions. Laura, unfortunately, destroyed her life with a continual series of selfish marriages, affairs, fights, and destructive monetary and relational choices. She chose her own way, not wisdom.

## Ask for Positive Changes

Moving past a fight often works best to boil down what you are trying to say into positive requests rather than negative accusations. People will be naturally defensive when you say, "Stop doing that," "I hate it when you do that," "I don't like that," or "It drives me nuts when you…." It is so much more helpful if you can think through the whole issue and find what you do want to happen. "Can we have dinner without the TV on?" "If you are going to be late, could you call me or text me." "Please give me as much warning as you can when you invite people over." "I just love it when you sit with me at church." "The kids are so excited when you come to their games." Like God asks us to pray for positives in Philippians 4:8 rather than dwell on the negative, marriages improve quickly when both husbands and wives can ask for the positive instead of declaring the negative they don't want.

Don't ask for something until you can ask for a positive. It might take a while to think about what you actually want, but it is worth this mental energy. Many husbands have found that they need to make notes on their phones or wherever while working through what they would like the issue to look like. You may not get all you want, but your wife can often add more to the positive picture you have painted. When you speak in positives rather than negatives, the whole relationship improves.

What are the positives you want in your home, at dinner time, in the evening, during the weekend, going to church, with the kids, visiting relatives, on vacations, with the budget, with political discussions, or with friendships? These are all areas where couples can have differences of opinion but can be discussed from the positive point of view rather than the negative.

## Growth Exercises—What Positive Action Can You Ask For?

What are three to four positive actions you would like to see in your marriage?

1. I want there to be time for just us.

2.

3.

4.

## Action Plan

One of the most delightful results of having a marriage that moves toward harmony is developing action plans with your spouse. Every project is an opportunity to work together. The goal is more love between you and your spouse, not accomplishing the project a certain way or at the lowest cost. When you have gone through the agreement system and come to a mutual decision, develop an action plan that is mutually agreed upon. It could be that you will delegate the project to an expert. It could be that one of the two of you is very capable of handling the new assignment or project. It could be that both of you will need to participate in this decision. Talk about the how not just the what. Use the agreement system to discuss the action plan just like you did to make the decision.

When there is constant talk or disappointment about a particular issue, it is time to develop an action plan. If it is clear that some action is needed, then one person must develop an action plan. What action plan will have the best chance of bringing about positive change or result? I have seen many spouses draw up action plans to try and wake up the other spouse about an issue. Usually, this involves going back through the agreement system with knowledgeable people about the spouse's reluctance to address this critical issue. As a godly husband, I have found that you must be willing to commit to a long time horizon for positive change (think one year, five years, ten years). At a certain point, issues like pornography, drinking, cheating, drugs, lying, violence, stealing, and so forth need action, not more talk. This could involve an intervention, reporting someone to the police, moving out, separation, significant restrictions, computer monitoring programs, and the like. Don't act until you have wise counsel, but also realize that pretending it will go away, in many cases, is naïve at best. Here are some questions I have asked when talking with the naïve husband or wife about their lack of an action plan:

What are you going to do if...?

What are you going to do to prepare for...?

When are you going to do the plan?

Who is advising you?

Will it get better if you do nothing?

———— ✺ ————

For a marriage that is going off the rails, here are some examples of actions you can take to heal the marriage:

Have the tough conversation

Call a counselor

Do the marriage exercises...things won't change without your participation.

Focus on the conversations, romantic times, and spending holidays together.

Help her out...it won't get better unless you do some of the small new things that will make it better.

Make changes...you can only change what you do.

Don't threaten...if it is time to act, then act.

Time travel...what would I change to bring about a different outcome?

I talked with a young lady years ago who told me that her husband had been violent with her one time during the first few years of their marriage. The wife developed an action plan to deal with this abuse, saving their marriage. She talked to the authorities and others, then had a meeting with him, telling him that in no uncertain terms, if anything like that ever happened again, the marriage would be over, and she would sue him for everything he had. She had gotten the right counsel and approached it in the right way, stopping the behavior in its tracks. I remember talking to her husband, and he said, "Oh, yes, it was clear she meant business. I realized that behavior could never happen again."

## Growth Exercises—Where Is an Action Plan Needed?

Are there any areas where an action plan is needed because talking has been exhausted and there doesn't seem to be any change taking place?

# PRINCIPLE #6—NURTURE

"So husbands ought also to love
their own wives as their own bodies.
He who loves his own wife loves himself;
for no one ever hated his own flesh,
but *nourishes and cherishes* it,
just as Christ also does the church."

Ephesians 5:28–29 (emphasis mine)

———∞———

**I** **have a confession to make.** I kill plants. I don't mean to, but I am horrible at remembering to water them. I never fertilize or weed around them. They die of neglect. I enjoy walking through a lush, beautiful garden, but I should not be put in charge of maintaining it. There was a time when I was single, and I treated people the same way. They will take care of themselves, I thought. I had to learn how to become a gardener of people and relationships before God trusted me with a real person to marry. It came as a shock to me that relationships need constant tending. People need emotional, mental, spiritual, and physical nutrients from the people around them, or else the relationship will die.

Many men treat their wives just like I treated my plants and the people in my life. They just assume she will be okay. "She is responsible for herself, and I am responsible for myself." This neglect-orientation has resulted in the death of many marriages. Neglecting your mate is choosing to value something else more than meeting her needs. You mistakenly believe she will always be around; she will survive. But, without the proper nutrients, her love for you will begin to die, and the marriage might not survive.

The reason we get married is that we are incomplete without our spouse. She can supply what we lack, and you can supply what she lacks. If both of you do your job, the relationship flourishes, and everybody lives happily ever after. She can win her personal battles with you by her side and vice versa. The place where your wife can grow into the fullness that God intended is within her marriage—if you treat her right.

You might think, "She doesn't need anything from me; she gets enough from the kids, friends, God, and the church. I can spend more time at work or on hobbies because that is what I like to do." This kind of thinking is totally wrong. She is not a forget-me-not flower.

Getting married can be like picking a beautiful flower or planting a beautiful rose garden. The choice is for the husband to make. One gives beauty for three days, and the other supplies beauty for a lifetime. Many men marry this lovely flower, then watch as it slowly shrivels and dies. He doesn't realize he took over maintenance of the flower from her father. If he provides nothing to keep the flower growing, he can't blame the woman for not being the lovely person he married. He caused this. The answer is not to get another flower but learn how to tend to your spouse.

When you committed to being your wife's husband, you became the *gardener* of the relationship. If the garden is in bad shape, we cannot blame the garden but the gardener. In other words, *your wife responds to the environment you create!* When your home life is not pleasant or helpful, the blame falls squarely at your feet. You make the environment your whole family lives in.

You, husband, are in a place to do something no one else can do for your wife. You can nourish your wife's deepest needs that no one else can meet. In general, she is not able to meet these needs herself. She is waiting for you to meet them. If you do not meet them, then she often wilts. On the other hand, if you take up the challenge and supply her with the nutrients she needs, she will blossom and develop into a dynamic, vibrant woman. She will become all that God intended her to be and reach way past what she or even you ever believed was possible.

A gentleman called recently in a state of panic. His wife had given him an ultimatum: either begin to treat her right or live somewhere else. He was totally shocked and indignant at this "line" his wife had drawn. He proclaimed his willingness to forsake all for his marriage, but he did not understand that his wife had different needs than he did. He believed she had the same needs, ambition, internal desires, and thoughts.

I assured him that his wife wanted a great marriage and was trying to tell him, "If you would begin to meet my needs, then the love we had at the beginning of the marriage could be possible again." He was totally unaware of how he was mistreating his wife. He felt he was almost a model husband. He bristled at the idea that there was something wrong with the way he was husbanding. Yet his wife was on the verge of throwing him out.

I find many men pour almost all of their energy, time, and creativity into their work life. Then they come home exhausted and have little left to give. Many men tell themselves that they work so hard for their family, but their family gets very little. Since your spouse is a higher priority relationship than your work, she deserves the best of you, not the dregs of what's leftover.

## What Does It Mean to Nuture Your Wife?

I want to introduce four specific needs that are most crucial to her thriving, and then we will delve into the things you can do to meet these needs.

Chapter 17—Meet Her Spiritual Need: Leadership

Chapter 18—Meet Her Mental Need: Communication

Chapter 19—Meet Her Emotional Need: Romance and Pursuit

Chapter 20—Meet Her Physical Need: Nonsexual, Tender Touch

# 17.

# MEETING HER SPIRITUAL NEED: LEADERSHIP

I can remember a man I worked with who was a very successful executive. He had lots of money but spent most of his time at the office. With all of the money he was making, He was not even aware that he was losing the relationship with his wife and the kids. I invited him to become a part of a godly husband class, and he accepted. He saw that he needed to lead his family completely differently. Scripture taught him that he needed to begin honoring his wife with time and compliments. He changed his schedule to be there at dinnertime and took Saturdays off. He began to understand what his wife needed, not just what he wanted. He poured into her and the children, and now he is universally acclaimed as a great husband and father. By the way, he also has a very successful business. He took this principle of nurturing his wife's spirit to heart, and it paid dividends. The great cry from most women is for their husbands to engage in helping lead the home. Don't give the best of yourself at work. Give the best you have to her and your family.

## Leading at Home

God has placed men as the head of the family, which means that you are responsible for finding the wisest course of action in each situation. Leadership at home does not mean you get to do what you want (called foolishness in Scripture). A godly husband is wise in finding the best course of action and the plan that allows the Triple Win (where God wins, others win, and you win). A simple definition of wise leadership is providing what is needed to go from here to there. This could be vision, energy, money, people, a plan, a relationship, etc. Most wives call this engagement at home.

Engaging at home will lead your wife, your kids, and the family toward what is best. Your leadership is not about what you want but what they need. You strive to help each of your children and your wife become fully developed as righteous people, making a righteous impact in society and loving each other. You must understand the team God has given you, then harness the team's unique talents, gifts, and abilities to be a force of positive change in the world.

Effective leadership involves four streams coming together to make a river, representing the health of the marriage and home. The stronger the four streams flow, the stronger the river, which signifies your leadership impact. When one of these streams gets stagnant or dammed up, the river of your family isn't as healthy. There isn't as much water flowing to make it as strong and robust as it could be. Let's take a look at the four streams and go from there.

### Stream 1—Doing the Expected

The first stream is basic—just do what you're supposed to do. I see many husbands complain about their wives resisting their leadership, and in many cases, they are right. If this is you, there's a good chance she is resisting because you are not doing what is expected. Think of it like this. If an employer hires people but never pays them, the employees would probably resist the boss's leadership. Paying the employees is a basic expectation.

In the same way, your wife expects and needs honor, understanding, security, building unity, an agreement system, and to be nurtured and defended, which you are learning to do. Consider these basics as the entrance tickets to the kind of marriage she expects. Without putting strategies in place to meet these basic needs, she will probably resist your leadership. However, as you learn and practice the scriptural principles laid out in this book, she will most likely warm to your leadership and flow of ideas because she knows they are not selfishly oriented.

Please spend some time discussing with your wife ten basic things she expects out of a husband. These are not things she would like you to do; these are things she expects you to do. You'll know what they are because if you do not do them, conflict ensues. Because of who her father is and how she was raised, she may expect you to do things you just can't do. If that is the case, you'll use your leadership to find a new or better way for those expected things to be done, even if it's not you.

## Growth Exercises—What Does Your Wife Expect of You?

Write down five things your wife expects you to do.

1. Take out the trash and replace the trash bag.

2.

3.

4.

5.

*Stream 2—Going Beyond the Expected*

To really captivate your wife's attention, you'll also want to go above and beyond the call of duty to inspire trust and followership. If you never initiate the special touches beyond what your wife expects, your marriage will settle into a business relationship. Many men avoid these things. They think that if they start doing more than the basics, their wife will expect it all the time. Many men try to keep their wife's expectations low. This is a failing strategy. You want her to have a number of things she can brag about to her friends about the unexpected things you do. "Matt was so sweet the other night. He left me a note saying he loved me on the counter." "Josh emptied the dishwasher while I was sleeping—I couldn't believe it!" Often these little extras take just a few minutes, but they boost your leadership and love in her eyes. Yes, you will have to go out of your way to do these things, but it is worth it.

Talk with your wife about ten things you could do that would be nice touches and pleasant surprises. Ask her not to be sarcastic. These would be wonderful or helpful to her—things that would be especially meaningful, and you would be met with, "You didn't have to do that, but thank you!"

## Growth Exercises—What Would Pleasantly Surprise Her?

Write down five things you could do that would pleasantly surprise your wife.

1. *Give her a day off from the kids.*

2.

3.

4.

5.

*Stream 3—She Needs to See You Leading*

The third stream of leadership demonstrates that you are taking the marriage and family somewhere. It is not enough to do the expected or even bless your wife with special touches. Your wife needs to know you have thought things through and have a plan for where the marriage and family are headed. What is our goal as a family? What is our mission? For your wife to see you clearly leading, you must do three things:

### 1. Provide a picture of the preferred future.

You must be able to describe to your wife what the marriage should look like in one, three, and five years, where you two should be living, and what life will be like there. This vision is not entirely yours; it comes in conjunction with your wife, wise counsel, and the Lord. Wives are usually very responsive when asked about their ideas regarding the future. She has opinions, ideas, and insights. I have found that writing down her responses to the various questions listed below is incredibly powerful. These will inform the "there" and allow everyone in the family to win. You are responsible for deciding which parts of the vision will be included and communicating the when, the how, and the why. If you don't do this, your marriage, family, and life will stagnate.

I realize there are some marriages where the wife is the engine powering the family to the preferred future. However, you must still take the role of filtering, steering, discussing, and incorporating all the family's needs. If your wife is a strong, natural leader, you are doubly blessed (look at the Proverbs 31 woman!), but you must still engage in this crucial aspect of leading your family. The great problem of our age is apathetic men who only lead outside the home. Your family needs your leadership. Get engaged and stay engaged.

Talk through these questions with your wife. The goal is to work together to develop an attractive vision of the future. What happens to many marriages is that the idealism and dreams of early marriage never get accomplished, and new dreams are not discussed to take their place. We need to repeat this exercise every year or two.

## Growth Exercises—Developing an Attractive Vision for the Future

1. Where do you think we should be living in…

   1 year?    3 years?    5 years?

2. What type of education or specialized training should we have in…

   1 year?    3 years?    5 years?

3. What type of careers do you think we should have in…

   1 year?    3 years?    5 years?

4. What do you think our family should be like in…

   1 year?    3 years?    5 years?

5. What types of vacations or places do we want to have experienced in…

   1 year?    3 years?    5 years?

6. What amount of yearly income should we be generating in…

   1 year?    3 years?    5 years?

7. What do you see our children doing in…

   1 year?    3 years?    5 years?

8. What types of hobbies and activities should we have become proficient in…

   1 year?    3 years?    5 years?

Remember that leadership is usually not linear in its accomplishment. There is an element of spontaneity. Rarely does a person detail the future and push relentlessly until it is accomplished. The accomplishments of our goals and dreams are a series of starts and serendipitous occurrences. When you have outlined the vision clearly, you can seize the opportunity to accomplish that vision once it comes along. If you had not detailed the vision in advance, the opportunity might have slipped by without notice. God often opens a door earlier or much later than we would have expected. When those doors open, it is crucial to be ready to move in that direction, made possible by preplanning.

### 2. Recruit the people to pull off the vision.

Many men are too stubborn to realize that if they are going to remodel the house, work two jobs, and spend time with their wives and kids, they are going to have to hire someone to do the remodeling. They believe they should be the ones to do it all. A good leader matches the job with the manpower needed for that job.

This includes figuring out what they need to accomplish the vision of the future life of the family. Each vision requires manpower, and the husband is responsible for developing and recruiting the people necessary to accomplish the picture of the preferred future. One of the most delightful assignments I ever engaged in was to project out five years for each of my children, then ask my wife, their teachers, and other parents what my kids could be doing, accomplishing, and enjoying five years from now. It helped me to see they were growing up and needed all kinds of experiences to do it well. Now, as I sit with them as adults, I enjoy asking them the same questions to get them thinking about where they want to be five years from now and how they can righteously maximize their lives.

### 3. Raise the money to accomplish the vision.

Another way to be clearly seen as a leader is to think through what amount of money and other resources it will take to achieve the shared vision of where the marriage and family need to go. Think through these questions, and go over them with your wife.

## Growth Exercises—Where Will the Resources Come From?

1. What sacrifices will we need to make to get there?

2. What changes will we need to make to accomplish the goal?
   - education
   - training
   - job changes
   - career moves

3. Where will the money come from?
   - work
   - savings and investments
   - gifts from others (including inheritance)
   - prayer that God opens up the windows of heaven because of the blessings He promises when we tithe

4. How can you both develop the above sources of income?
   - work
   - savings and investments
   - gifts
   - prayer/tithing

In many marriages, both the wife and husband have different views of where the money will come from and how it will be spent. Does he think she will work? Does he never want her to work? What will any extra money go toward? Does he plan on starting his own business someday? Where will he get the startup money? Will he work two jobs or more? Does she think his presence is more important than a little extra money? How much will be saved out of each paycheck? How much money will go toward making life comfortable now? Does he want to keep working at his present job until he retires? What other career fields have you considered? What standard of living do you want in retirement? What sources of income will you live off in your retirement years? Have you thought about the significant needs that will push you forward in your late forties and early fifties?

It's helpful to develop a plan as to how you will maximize your income and giving to glorify God to the fullest extent capable. It is helpful to talk to a financial planner, a good tax man, and wise, successful people in these areas. It is also beneficial to take a basic family financial course. There are several out there. Dave Ramsey's Financial Peace University is a beneficial course.

### Stream 4—Mentoring Others

Good leaders lead, and one of the ways to do this is by becoming a mentor. When your wife sees you as someone wise enough that other people are willing to listen to your counsel and wisdom, it elevates your leadership in her eyes. The more people she sees looking to you and listening to you, the more she will allow you to lead her. Mentoring is not having people follow you. Mentoring is having people voluntarily follow you to gain your insights and knowledge. It means that people grow in their ability to handle some aspects of life by being with you.

One of the easiest ways to get started in mentoring is to offer to host a small group at your church. You can invite friends from church or start in the youth department having a small group of young people. We often learn most when we prepare to communicate with others. Invite people over, have some snacks, and discuss how to live out the sermon preached at church. Find a video series that people might be interested in, then watch it and lead a discussion. It is incredible how hosting a group, praying for others, and asking questions to get the conversation started will encourage people to seek your wisdom.

This also means your wife needs to see the children and others coming to you for advice. If you make time to be with people, they want to be with you and gain your truth. Ask God to direct you to people who could benefit from your wisdom and insight.

### Growth Exercises—Are You Called to Mentorship?

- Who are you mentoring?
- Who might want a piece of your knowledge?
- Which friends will never listen to your counsel?
- Who could you help the most?

## Leading Her Spirit

Leading your wife's spirit well means you must first understand her spirit. If you can grasp the unique way your wife experiences life, it will make a huge difference. By now you realize that she is completely different from you. She does not see the world through your lenses. Understanding her spirit will be like doing original research on the most amazing person in your life. Abdicating or ignoring this process leaves the marriage and family without a male leader.

Part of understanding your wife's spirit is to grasp how to strengthen, encourage, and direct her for her own best interest, the family's best interest, and society's best interest. The spirit is a complex structure made up of immaterial dimensions, along with the soul (mind, will, and emotions). The following is a list of the aspects of a person's spirit: conscience; originality/creativity (self-expression); connection to God; personality; security; significance; leadership and followership.

## Growth Exercises—How Can You Lead Her Spiritually?

1. How have you demonstrated sensitivity to your wife's and your *conscience*? Have you pushed her past her moral comfort level? In what areas?

2. How have you demonstrated your *originality and creativity*? In what ways have you given room for your wife to express her originality and creativity? In what areas have you squelched her self-expression?

3. How have you demonstrated a regular and vital *connection to God*? What are the ways she connects most deeply with God? How have you led her to a more vital connection to God? Have you held her back from connecting with God in any way?

## Growth Exercises—How Can You Lead Her Spiritually?

4. How have you demonstrated the strengths of your *personality* and a growing handle on the non-strengths of your personality? How have you encouraged your wife to develop and express her strengths? What actions have you taken to shield or protect her areas of non-strength?

5. How have you demonstrated *security* in who you are and the part God wants you to play in life? How have you helped your wife develop growing security and assurance in who she is? How have you encouraged her that she does not have to do all things well, only the areas where God has gifted her?

6. How have you demonstrated the balance of gaining *significance* from your work and relationships? How have you developed your wife's ability to sense her significance through increased depth of relationship and competence in skills? Is it clear to your wife that you consider her incredibly significant?

7. How have you demonstrated submission to those in *leadership* above you? Are you a good follower? How have you shown your wife how to appeal a decision without rebellion? Does your wife understand the difference between creative submission, rebellion, and doormat thinking?

# 18.
## MEETING HER MENTAL NEED:
## COMMUNICATION

W hat is one of the biggest needs of your wife? Emotional Intimacy through intimate conversations. Most guys want physical intimacy. Most ladies want emotional intimacy. The mental aspect of your wife's life is complex and varies from woman to woman. However, almost all women have a deep, abiding need to connect verbally in a meaningful way every day.

We all have mental needs, such as knowledge, planning, mental framework, and so on. Still, your wife's most important need in the marriage is fulfilling her mental need, which is achieved through deep, interactive communication. This is way more than just talking. She wants you to hear her feelings, concerns, ideas, and dreams and for you to interact with them. She doesn't want you to dismiss them but engage with them. She needs to know that her most sacred thoughts and feelings are safe with you, that you will understand and guide her to new ways of thinking about these very real ideas. This is what having an intimate friend means to her.

If your wife doesn't get this type of communication from you, she will look for it in others, even with another man, if that's who meets this need in her (could be her father, a pastor, your friends, her boss, co-workers, a neighbor, someone she meets at the gym, and so forth). Many of these people are not safe sources for this kind of inti- macy, and all of them are poor substitutes for the deep, interactive communication she should be having with you, her husband.

According to Carolyn Hax, advice columnist for the Washington Post, "Many wives have husbands who are conversational narcissists." She does not believe that some men will ever be interested in what their wives are talking about. They only want to talk about what they are interested in. In her line of work, women are always pouring their hearts out to her about the fact that their husbands never ask them any questions, ever. These husbands never forget about their own thoughts and they never follow up their wives' statements with questions. It is this self-focus that robs them of the deep affection and trust of their wives.[14] *But godly husbands are not like this.* A godly husband realizes that his wife's ideas and feelings are crucial to building a friendship with her. Only when the husband understands her and nurtures her by listening and interacting will she feel fulfilled in this area.

Every day I set aside at least an hour to listen to and talk with my wife. I have meetings all day with people, but this is my second most important meeting, right after my meeting with God. I've learned that my ability and willingness to meet with my wife determine my marriage's health. I personally do not *need* this meeting every day, but my wife does. I know when she is listened to and talked with and knows that I know what is going on with her, she is an energized woman.

Many men avoid this type of meeting because they do not need to talk and be listened to this much. But your wife is different from you. This kind of interaction is like super-grow fertilizer to her soul. Embrace her need for this type of communication and watch your wife and marriage thrive. All it takes is your focused attention for one hour every day. Just embrace this meeting like you embrace the need for sleep. It has to happen. There are so many times when I have just listened to my wife's concerns or events of the day, and she exclaims, "I feel so much better!" when it is over, even though I have not offered solutions or talked all that much except to ask questions about her concerns.

The kind of communication that meets her mental need is deep, interactive, regular, and extensive. It must exhibit certain qualities and not just quantity. Most men can live perfectly fine with very little of this type of communication. For them, task-oriented information is just fine but know this—engaging your wife in this way will enrich your marriage beyond measure. "Deep, interactive communication" can be defined like this:

1.  It is **deep** because it is about the inner person, not just what you or your wife do from day to day. It involves exploring the deepest parts of your wife's thoughts, emotions, and spirit. Your wife has new ideas every day. She experiences new feelings all the time. She interacts with the world through the various aspects of her spirit, soul, and body. All of this may be largely hidden from her and will take time to uncover. She wants to tell you about her feelings and her thoughts. Rejoice in this. When she doesn't want to tell you is when your marriage is really in trouble.

2.  It is **interactive** because it involves listening to her thoughts, emotions, ideas, and concerns and responding by sharing your own thoughts, emo-

tions, and ideas with her. She needs you to explain who you are to her and why you act and think the way you do. She needs you to listen to her and follow her as she goes in a number of different directions in a single conversation. It is a dialogue, not a monologue. She needs to interact with you, not just recite a list of her emotions. Your comments and ideas need to be mixed into her thoughts, feelings, and desires to create an entirely new set of thoughts, feelings, and desires.

3.  It is **communication** because there must be understanding and reactions or responses. Communication is more than just hearing words and nodding, and more than just telling facts. It is getting involved with the other person, seeking to understand their thoughts, feelings, and actions. *It responds to her ideas, not spring-boarding to your thoughts or topics.* Think about what she is saying and be willing to stay with a conversation until actual communication (understanding) has taken place.

Your wife needs about an hour of this type of communication every single day of her life. If she does not get it, she will be loaded for bear on Saturday and Sunday, having built up a backlog of things to talk about. Do not treat your marriage as a business relationship and expect her to get by. She needs you to talk to and listen to her.

## Catch-and-Release Fishing

One illustration that has proven helpful for many husbands contemplating really loving their wives through deep, interactive communication is catch-and-release fishing. Many men are aware of the thrill of casting a lure on the water and having a big game fish chomp on the bait and then take off. The fish is trying to get away, and you are trying to reel it in without breaking the line. After ten to thirty minutes, you reel in the fish and hold it up for a photo before releasing it back into the wild.

This analogy shows how these important conversations with your wife work. Your wife has huge emotional and mental thoughts (fish) inside her head, and your job is to fish for them. You may not want to, but let me help you learn to enjoy it. First, you throw out a line by asking questions about what happened in the day and how she felt, and soon a huge emotional fish will bite on the question, and you are off the races. She wants to talk more about this. You ask more questions. You are trying to reel in the emotional or mental fish, and she is just letting it run. She is looking for clues about if you really want to land (understand) what she is talking about and why it is important to her.

When you are fishing, you don't analyze why the fish went this way or that way; you just try to stay with it to land this sucker. It is the same with talking and listening to your wife. Stop analyzing why she is saying this or that or what it might mean for your chore list, and just try and land (understand) this mental or emotional fish. This can be great fun for you and her if you can see it as something that fills her up. She needs you to be interested in these emotional and mental fish hatched during the day, the week, and the month. She wants you to ask questions, follow her train of thought, and listen intensely while trying to understand what this is all about. She needs you to really show you love her by thoroughly engaging in the listening in the same way you would trying to land a ten-pound trout. She wants you to land the emotional or mental fish and show it to her. "Is this what you were feeling or trying to say?" When she says, "Yes, that is what I was feeling!" or "Yes, that is what I was thinking," you've landed the fish and can release it. Success!

She will often release three to five fish during an hour of conversation with you. Imagine what fun it would be to have three to five big game fish on the line during an hour of fishing! This is what listening to your wife is like. I realize her emotions can be scary and unpredictable to you, and that is maybe why you don't want to go fishing for them in the first place. But she needs you to get into the game of really loving her by catch-and-release fishing for her emotions.

Too many guys are trying to contemplate what this emotion means for them or what this new wild idea will mean they have to do. Stop doing that and just enjoy the process of fishing. She may not know what her thoughts mean; she just knows she is anxious, angry, has a new idea for the den, or is worried about your youngest child. Psychologists tell us that we have processed it when we can get an idea out of our heads and explain it fully to another person. This is what your wife needs you to do for her daily. She is hatching emotional and mental fish every day, and she needs someone to understand them so she can process them. She needs someone committed enough to listen and fight to understand what this is all about. Ninety to 95 percent of the time, there is no action required beyond listening and understanding. This is what it means to really love your wife. Enjoy it and watch your marriage improve.

What does this practically look like? Let me walk you through the process.

*To start fishing, throw out a lure:*

Ask her what happened during the day.

Don't settle for "it was fine." You want specifics: who, when, where, what, how. (Your engagement here is what tells her you love her.)

Ask two to three questions about every item she talks about.

When she starts talking more about an incident, a feeling, an idea, or a person, the chase begins. (She has chomped the lure; she is ready to tell you more if you will keep this topic on the line.)

*To keep the fish (topic) on the line, do these things:*

Keep asking questions.

Look directly at her, and make eye contact.

Give her minimal encouragers, like nodding your head, grunting, or making quick comments. ("Uh-huh," "Tell me more," "You don't say," "Well, that's interesting.")

*Start reeling in the fish by doing these things:*

Ask, "Is this (_____) what you feel?"

Paraphrase what you have heard.

Follow her train of thought or words even if it doesn't make sense to you.

Stop trying to make sense of these ideas or feelings in your world.

Summarize what you heard her say.

When she says, "Yes, that is what I was feeling!" or "Yes, that is what I was thinking," you've caught the fish, and it's now in the boat.

*Show her the fish, then release it. Prepare to catch another fish by casting out another lure.*

Many of these catch and release fishing episodes are quick, maybe five to ten minutes. She will often release another fish and see if you are ready to fish for that.

Your wife might have three to five fish that she wants to have you fish for every day. Then she would like to fish for your own emotional and mental fish, as she knows you also hatch emotional and mental fish that need to be caught and released. This whole process of catch-and-release communication can be a gratifying process for both of you. Give it a try!

Husbands tell me, "I talk with my wife every day." But unless there are emotions, ideas, and vulnerability, it is not the kind of communication that will minister to her deepest needs. I tend to see it as my most important counseling appointment. "How did your day go?" "Any highlights?" "What was the most interesting thing that happened to you today?" "Start from the beginning and tell me everything about the day." Anything she brings up, I ask at least two to three questions about it: that person, that event, her feelings, her concerns, and so on. This always creates a conversation that could go in several directions.

## What Deep, Interactive Communication Is

*It is an internal journey.*

This explores feelings, goals, desires, inner thoughts, personal tension, fears, dilemmas, wisdom, and the inner journey. Your wife needs to know that she knows the "you" on the inside and can reveal herself to you without any fear of rejection.

Such quality communication exposes who you are in the inner person and allows her to expose herself. This process is not like what takes place in a counseling office, where someone pours out their insides for an hour. The process and your wife's need are that, over time, both of you would have revealed yourselves to each other in small, bite-sized pieces. This time-lapsed revelation causes the person to come into focus only over time. It also gives the other person the ability to change and grow in the inner person.

*It is the creation of a climate of acceptance.*

This means that you both feel the freedom to share sensitive material with the other person without feeling like it will come back during a disagreement or cause the other person to pull away. The ability to create this climate of acceptance is dependent on your ability as a husband to act like Christ and offer unconditional love. If your wife senses you cannot forgive or you will not understand, she will not share. Build a climate of acceptance in your marriage and especially when you talk. She can tell you anything, and you won't be upset or distance yourself from her.

Caution: There may be events, people, thoughts, and feelings that you or your wife cannot share because it is too raw or damaging. These things can and should be shared with a counselor or a pastor. Do not assume your spouse can share everything with you or you with her. This is a goal in marriage, but it may take a long while to get there. Just keep making progress, and before you know it, you will be hearing and revealing thoughts and feelings in a climate of acceptance you would have never dreamed was possible. What George Washington Carver said about plants can apply to interpersonal communications: Love anything enough, and it will yield its secrets to you.

Also, some women need less of this than others. Each woman's temperament is different, and some women need less of this deep type of conversation. However, they do still need it. Interestingly, the women who need it less are usually married to men who can give much more of it.

## What Deep, Interactive Communication Is Not

*It is not a conversation about the weather, activities of the day, or news.*

These may be the starting point for communication. However, talking with your wife about these areas does not meet this need. Deep, interactive communication in the way your wife needs involves sharing your thoughts, feelings, dreams, goals, fond memories, and nightmares and listening to her on these same themes. Your initial, more superficial conversation can bring these deeper themes to mind.

*It is not task communication about work, to-do lists, or technical data.*

These areas are the usual extent of a man's conversation. He is quite comfortable in the concrete world of tasks. His wife is not interested in the task, per se. She wants to know what's behind the task—the instructions and interactions. She knows that the task information is important, but it is only the beginning of the communication, not the whole of it.

Notice how much your wife perks up when you begin to share personal information about the people you work with and the behind-the-scenes reasons a directive came down. This is the information she needs to connect with your world and feed her soul. Be careful that you do not break any confidences or slip into gossip when sharing any information.

## Typical Communication Patterns

### Floating Trial Balloons First

A woman's typical communication pattern is the exact opposite of a man's. A man will exchange pleasantries and then get to the main point quickly. "The reason I called is…" or "I want to talk with you about…." After the big issue or main point has been taken care of, then and (usually) only then, can there be a discussion of all the other little bits of information, which are unrelated but could be discussed with this person.

A woman's pattern starts with the same exchange of pleasantries but then begins to wander to seemingly unrelated bits of information. At times, there seems to be no real point to all the talk. This usually means your wife has a topic in the background she wants to talk to you about, but she wants to check and make sure if you are in a good listening mood before she brings it up. She is floating up trial balloons to see if you'll engage. In her mind, she thinks if you do not listen to the little bits of information, you will not listen when she tells you something really important.

Unfortunately, this pattern usually convinces men that there is no point in their wives' communication. He might even conclude that she will continue to drivel on like this for hours, never coming to any point. This is not the case! Husbands must realize that the climate of acceptance they create is the only way to speed up the process of their wives taking a risk and talking about what is really on their hearts.

In the beginning, you cannot hurry her along to get to the point. Even if you talk about this seemingly random information, she has to sense that you are actually listening before she will give you the big piece of news. *You just need to listen.* After a while, as you have demonstrated the ability to listen and really care about what she says, she will be open to revealing the point. Sure, she can get to the point with a trusted girlfriend quickly. But you want her to be the one she opens up to. She will be able to get to the point quickly with you when she trusts you are listening. You cannot order her to get to the point. It will not work. She needs to run up her trial balloons first.

### Painting Pictures

Your wife can do something that most men stopped doing when they became teenagers. She can actually picture a situation she has never been in if given enough details. This is called visualization. The fact that she is trying to paint a picture is why she asks so many questions. She must glean enough data from you to know how to paint the picture.

Men, in general, cannot visualize or desire to paint a picture of their wife's day.

This leads to many men becoming resentful of all the questions their wives ask. He says that he had a conversation with Bob. She wants a detailed description of what each person said and what Bob was wearing at the time.

This is not something to be resisted as intrusive or irritating. Instead, it should be welcomed as a way for your wife to participate with you to enter your world and understand how you think and act. She believes that you know these details, and they provide a much more appealing conversation to her.

When you say you had a conversation with Bill, she wants to know whether you were standing or sitting. Where did the conversation take place? Did either of you have anything in your hands? Was anyone else listening or standing around? Did Bill look interested or distant? At any point, were you interrupted? What did you say precisely? Did you get the feeling that Bill was listening? Did you get to the main point? How did you end the conversation?

All these and many other questions are what goes through her mind. She is trying to participate with you in your life. She is your life partner. This is why a woman can spend a whole day with another lady and then get on the phone and talk about the day with her. She wants all these questions answered as if she was there.

You may not ever get into this picture-painting process to the measure that another woman might tend to, but you must understand that your wife needs this detail to help fulfill her life with you. She wants to have you as her best friend. It is also important that she has close and trusted girlfriends with whom she can fully engage in this type of activity.

## Overreacting to Ideas

Because of their ability to visualize, most women cannot listen to a new idea without hearing all the ramifications that idea has on them. When a man comes home and says he is thinking about moving to Montana, his wife begins to try to live in Montana mentally. If this is not a picture she likes, then she reacts negatively.

It is often important to precede any new idea with statements that let her know these are just thoughts and that you have no intention of acting on these thoughts without a great deal of talking and counsel. There needs to be some way to signal your wife to relax and discuss this new thought with you. Help her understand that a man explains himself while explaining his thoughts. He discloses who he is when he describes the ideas that get him excited.

Because women can overreact to a new or different idea, they often push their men away. As the husbandman in the home, help her not to overreact. You can push through her poor response and continue to explain yourself. If she overreacts to a new idea, begin the discussion so that she can listen and enter into the conversation.

### Focusing on People

Most women find information about people more interesting than facts. They are more captivated by relational details than by horsepower or firepower. This means that if a man is to keep his wife interested in his topics, he must share the relational and personal information that would cause her to care. She may not care about football, but she might care about how a football player is trying to save his marriage, deal with his autistic child, or care for his aging mother.

The human interest or difficult obstacles in a person's life are fascinating to your wife. She does not care how many widgets you produced, but she would be interested in Jack almost slugging Bill during the final stages of production of those widgets. Nearly all situations have human-interest angles. Unless only robots are involved, there will be interesting people. Those people have hopes, dreams, problems, and pain. The "people" aspect will allow her to become interested in what you are interested in.

## Communicate to Build Your Friendship

When a person (man or woman) shares the deeper parts of themselves—their thoughts, feelings, desires, goals, and so forth—they are drawn into a more profound love with the person willing to listen to them. The fact that the other person heard your innermost things and still listens and wants to be with you likely releases a new level of love for this person. (By the way, this is how mistresses usually operate and affairs begin, so beware.)

When a person feels they can share their deepest feelings and thoughts with another person, they feel they have found a "best friend." Many married couples long to be closer and enjoy a deep friendship with their spouse, but they do not know how to get there. These listening and talking skills that makeup communication are the pathways to making your spouse your best friend.

### Listening Skills

#### Eye Contact

The most positive thing you can do for a person talking to you is to look at them. Nothing says you are paying attention and want to listen like looking the person in the eye. Of course, there are exceptions, like when you are in bed, and the lights are turned off or driving in the car! Most men get into trouble when their wives are talking because they simultaneously try to watch TV or read the newspaper, play on the computer or video game, or work on the car. Make eye contact to show you are engaged and ready to listen.

### Minimal Encouragers

These are the little sounds, words, and gestures you use to say, "Tell me more," without interrupting the person. These would include "uh-huh," "Yes, I hear you," "Really? No!" "You don't say!" "Well, I'll be!" and so forth. Gestures would include nodding the head, leaning forward, moving the hands, and so on.

### Parroting/Mirroring/Reflecting Back

This is a constructive way of encouraging people to talk, even though it seems very strange when you first use it. This is where you take the same word or sentence that the other person used and repeat it back exactly as they said it.

Wife: "I feel so frustrated!"

Husband: "It sounds like you're feeling frustrated."

At first, this seems like it would irritate the other person, but when it is done with a desire to listen rather than to mock, it will almost always cause the other person to elaborate on their feelings. Then you can parrot those back and go even deeper.

### Paraphrasing

Instead of parroting back exactly what was said, this is where you give another word or phrase in its place. This is very helpful and causes the listener to think about what was said and check and see if they got it right.

### Summary Statements

This is probably the most helpful means of saying to another person, "I am listening." A person will usually pause after a period of talking. This is where you can summarize what you think you heard.

An example would be: "I think I heard you talk about three different things. Let me see if I got this right. You feel discouraged when you are angry because this causes you to think about your mother."

Often the other person will want to add to your summarization content they failed to mention the first time through. Plus, this lets them know that what you heard was not what they said or meant or if you heard the right emphasis on the words and phrases they used. Many times, husbands and wives argue and miscommunicate because one of the spouses will seize upon a particular word in what was said and argue, "But you said...." We must allow others to correct a poor choice of words or an inappropriate or unintended tone or attitude.

### The Timing of Good Listening

Invariably, one partner is wide awake in the morning and sleepy at night, while the other person is against mornings and ready to solve the world's problems after 11:00 p.m. These two people will never be able to carry on a conversation at their peak times, but they should learn to compromise by scheduling the talk time at their secondary peak times. Good timing matters when you want to discuss important topics.

### Points of View

Men typically don't want or appreciate advice or solutions when they are depressed or have lost a job. Sometimes they just want to mope for a while, and the last thing they want their wife to do is come in and tell them how to solve the problem. Women can relate—this is how she feels all the time! "Just listen to me and support me from my point of view. Don't try and help me understand my adversary's point of view. If I need to change my point of view, then I will do it. I don't want you to become an advocate for anyone but me."

### Talking Skills

### Prefixes

This skill involves starting each sentence with something like, "I feel," or, "It seems," rather than, "You feel...You did...You didn't...You always...You never...They didn't." When we make a judgment about someone else at the beginning of a sentence, the other party is put on the defensive, and communication is cut down or off.

### Escape Clauses

This is a follow-up to the idea of prefixes. Escape clauses give people room to wiggle out of something they said or did. You can start statements with phrases like, "I don't know whether you meant to, but... It seems that I heard... Did I hear correctly...? You might want to consider... I don't know whether this has any value to you, but... I'm not really sure that... You can disagree with me, but... I can clearly see why someone would do that, but can I point out why that might not be the best alternative?" Each of these phrases gives the listener the ability to disagree or agree without feeling condemned. Interestingly, the more room the person feels to disagree, the more often they will not.

### No Psychoanalysis of Motives

One of the great dangers of talking with someone we have been around for a while is that we can begin to think we really know why that person did a particular thing. We are often wrong, and we always offend them when we say, "The reason you did that was..." or "You always do that because...(your mother, you're insecure, you still feel guilty about...)."

Many husbands traditionally try and stereotype their wives with comments about their motives. Many wives have given up defending themselves because the man will not listen. This reinforces the husband's thinking that his wife's silence means he is right. Even if he is right (he usually is not), guessing at the motives kills communication and rarely causes any changes. Give up this pseudo-psychoanalysis.

### No Labels

The names and derogatory remarks given to women (because they do not do things the way we would) can destroy a marriage and push our wives away from us. Words such as, "I can't believe anybody could be so dumb ... stupid, stupid, stupid... lazy; you are just plain lazy ... don't you ever think? ... do you have anything up there?" There are hundreds of labels and sarcastic digs that we can use as cute phrases or spears in an argument, but they are about as helpful as a Jell-O telephone when you have a 9-1-1 marital emergency. Stay away from offensive labels and derogatory remarks.

### Risk-taking

Getting good communication going involves one person taking some risks and revealing parts of themself. These thoughts pop into our minds when talking to another person—thoughts that show a deeper, inner side to who we are. We must begin to share some of these. Only when we take such risks can we move forward in our relationships with our wives.

### Encouragement and Praise

We should regularly share all the positive and encouraging thoughts or feelings we have about them with our mates. If something strikes you as particularly helpful or sacrificial, do not hold it back—share it! Catch them doing something good. If you think, "Boy, she looks beautiful," or "I really love her!" let her know. Also, leave love notes around the house for her to find.

### Identify Feelings, Thoughts, Dreams, and Goals

Begin identifying those deep parts of yourself and talk about them. This will be very difficult for most men and exceedingly difficult for extremely private people. Over time, with the help of a supportive wife, you can begin to understand your own feelings and thoughts better than you ever thought possible. If you include your wife in the exploration, you will be amazed at how close the two of you can become.

### Withhold Damaging Information and Topics

There are some topics that your wife cannot handle you talking about. Some she will be able to take later as you build a climate of acceptance and love for her. Some topics will always be taboo (such as premarital sexual encounters or partners). These might need to be shared with a mature friend, a counselor, or a pastor only.

All of the above ideas and techniques are ways to improve your marriage. God made humans in a way that they must talk to truly communicate. We cannot read minds. We cannot assume we know what people are thinking or feeling. We need to ask them and then listen to what they say. I have trained hundreds of men on being more engaged listeners to their wives. Everyone can do it. It is just a matter of whether their marriage is important enough to do it.

In some marriages, the man needs all of this talking and listening as much as or more than the wife. If this is true for you, then rejoice because you can understand what she needs. Enjoy the marriage you are in and learn the unique features of your wife's needs. She's different from you, but she can be understood by learning to communicate intimately and deeply.

## Growth Exercises—Talking and Listening Skills

1. Set aside an hour for each of the five days this next week to talk with your wife.

2. Go catch-and-release fishing for the emotional and mental fish that hatch in your wife's life every day.

3. Make a list of topics you can discuss. Try for twenty items.

   - Ask her about her day.
   - Ask her about the kids.
   - Ask her about her work.
   - Ask her about her friends.
   - Ask her about a church event or group.
   - Ask her about her concerns about the city, state, or nation.
   - Ask her about her dreams.
   - Ask her about vacation ideas.
   - Ask her about what she wants to save for or enjoy.
   - Ask her about her quiet time or walk with God.

4. Practice the listening and talking techniques in this chapter each day.

   - Ask questions
   - Make eye contact
   - Minimal encouragers
   - Verbally follow
   - Paraphrase her emotions or ideas
   - Summarize the ideas and emotions

# 19.

## MEETING HER EMOTIONAL NEED: ROMANCE AND PURSUIT

"Draw me after you and let us run together!"
Song of Solomon 1:4a NASB

─────⊛⊛⊛─────

**S**arah left a note on the refrigerator and was gone. She could no longer take his insensitivity. Roger would come home, plop in front of the TV, and wait until dinner. "He doesn't even always greet me. His world revolves totally around him. I can't remember the last time he took me out. I can no longer take the insensitive comments he throws at me. I am still a woman and deserve to be treated with respect. I want to have him come after me, to want to be with me like he did years ago. Now our whole life is the kids and how tired he is."

Thankfully, Roger was willing to listen to what Sarah was saying. I explained to him what it was she needed from him. He was more than willing to work at his marriage; he just didn't know it was in trouble. Roger had perfectly designed his marriage to meet his needs but had not considered that Sarah might also have needs. Roger, like many husbands, thought that her needs were the same as his or that she would make sure her own needs were met. After a few weeks of dating Sarah and giving her the honor she deserved, she was back home and renewed in her love for this man. She even began telling the other women at church about where her wonderful husband had taken her on their dates.

Your wife has a deep need to be romanced. This may mean little to you, but it is a huge component of her life. She needs to be pursued. She needs to be made to feel special. She needs to see at least weekly that life will get better or has the hope of getting better in the future. She needs to know that she is worth going out of your way for, that you enjoy spending time with her, or that you're willing to meet some need she has.

Let's face it. You tend to pursue the people you need, like, and enjoy. You pursue their time and wisdom; you go to them for fun or to listen and get feedback. Your wife needs to experience you doing that with her too.

Some men don't need romance. They are only interested in the conquest, not the hunt. They mistakenly (perhaps subconsciously) reason, "If I have already married this person, why should I still hunt her? Haven't I already won the big trophy?" Realize that your wife has an immense need to be romanced and pursued. Make it a part of your life to meet this need every week.

Romance for a woman is different than it is for a man. For a man, it tends to be a prelude to sex. He is usually unsure why romance needs to come before physical intimacy, but he realizes it is true. Most men are linear and goal-oriented and are willing to add elements to accomplish the goal. This pragmatic use of romance looks pretty selfish and mechanical to most women because they see romance differently. Sarah longed to be romanced—to be pursued. She wanted Roger to want to be with her—to talk with her, listen to her, enjoy being in her presence, have fun, and connect at a soul level. To her, dinner and a movie were not a part of a formula for getting sex at the end of the night. The date needed to be more than that.

## What Is Romance to a Woman?

Your wife needs romance because she sees her world relationally, not just with a task or goal to be checked off. To her, romance is being pursued by you. You want to be with her. You want to know what she thinks. You want to hear her laugh and enjoy being in your company. You want to enjoy the whole person of who she is.

A more technical definition of romance is going out of your way to know her and provide some hope for a better future. A weekly date night will likely do the trick, whether on the weekend or even a night during the middle of the week. Scheduling it to be on the same day each week helps men avoid letting weeks go by without one.

The key thing about a date is the pursuit of her, not the amount of money spent. This is a chance to do more catch-and-release fishing in your wife's soul. She sees this as a time when you want to spend time with her to be known. A date should be enjoyable for both parties, and it should re-energize and deeply encourage both people.

It should be fun and doesn't need to be overly complicated or expensive. Most men believe that a date should end with a sexual encounter because this is the most fun they can think of. Realize that your wife is hoping for an emotional and relational encounter through listening, talking, laughing, and learning, which will energize her to want the sexual encounter too.

## Growth Exercises—Planning a Date Night

1. Write down what day and time each week you could dedicate to spending time with your wife on a date.

2. Plan the first date night with her in mind. Where will you go? What will you do? How much money do you want to spend?

## Romance Is the Goal

The above definition of romance points out that romance is an end in itself. It is not trying to achieve something else or some other goal. Romance *is* the goal. Romance says to her, "My husband sees me as an interesting person who is a delight to his soul. He wants to pursue my soul, not just my body. He wants to know what I think, what I have been through, what I am feeling."

Romance provides the incredible hope created by enjoying the finer things in life. The encouragement comes from having her husband treat her as special, using every means to declare that she is on a pedestal in his life. *This is romance for a woman.* It is a need she has to get filled by her husband and is not optional. If she does not receive weekly doses of romance, she will become emotionally closed to you. When that happens, she becomes less alluring and unable to open up. She also begins to pull back on the dreams that have been so much a part of her life. Her husband's love should truly be the wind beneath the wings of her dreams.

In defense of men, many simply do not need to be romanced. Therefore, they cannot feel the need to "do this thing called romance." Many husbands view romance as an introductory price to pay for sexual intimacy, so they remain baffled by their wife's increasing irritation about their "dates."

Remember, a date is not a romantic encounter unless you have gone out of your way to spend time with your wife, communicating that you are still interested in her, that she is still a person worth pursuing. You are willing to invest time, money, and energy to be with your wife. Believe me when I say that she reads these clues, or the lack of them, as evidence of how valuable she is to you.

## Growth Exercises—Adjust Your Expectations for Sex

Next time you go on a date with your wife, try to adjust your expectations about the night ending in sexual intimacy. Just try it once and watch what happens.

## Romance Means Going Out of Your Way for Her

A woman has an emotional need to know she is significant enough for a man to go out of his way to spend time with her, understand her, and pursue her insides. This is not a desire, fantasy, or desire—*it is a need*. This is the emotional demonstration of honoring her as number one in your life. She needs to see you go out of the way as a demonstration that you highly prize her.

Planning the date dramatically increases your wife's sense of romance. If you turn to your wife as you go out the door and say, "What do you want to do tonight?" she knows you have not gone out of your way to even think about the evening. It is best to let your wife know what you plan a few days ahead. Sometimes you can give her three options and ask her what she wants to do.

Going out of your way could also mean arranging for the behind-the-scenes activities. This might mean calling to arrange the babysitter. This could involve calling for reservations at the restaurant. This might mean mapping out the location or checking the times for the movies, or purchasing anything that will be needed during the date ahead of time (tickets, food, cards, coats, seat cushions, etc.).

Another example of going out of the way could mean making the beginning of the date special with cards, notes, flowers, or candy. When special touches are added, these communicate that you have planned and are interested in being with your wife and making her happy.

And finally, going out of your way might mean including things your wife would like in the date even though you might not enjoy it. She will be aware of your sacrifice and encouraged that you are aiming to please her.

**Growth Exercises—Getting Creative with Your Dates**

1. What are 5 dates you could plan today?
2. What are 5 behind-the-scenes arrangements you could make?
3. What are 5 special beginning-of-the-date touches you could do?
4. What are 5 things you could include on the date that would demonstrate to your wife that you consider her ideas, desires, and likes?

## Romance Means Pursuing Her as a Person

This is one of the essential ingredients in the process of romance. Often, dates are planned to meet this romantic need, but remember, this is a time to pursue the person, not just to do something fun. If the activity ends and there has been no greater understanding of your wife or valuing her, it has not been a romantic time. It has been just a fun time. Your dates were valuable for romance when you were younger because they were used for learning about the person's mental, emotional, spiritual, and physical state. They still need to be used in this way all the years later.

Let me emphasize how important the idea of soul connection and emotional connection is to the health of your marriage. The concepts discussed in the "Deep, Interactive Communication" portion of chapter 18 are the heart of a great date for your wife. She needs you to want to explore her new feelings, new ideas, dreams, and concerns in a more extended platform, free from the distraction of the kids. A significant part of your date will be catch-and-release fishing for emotional and mental fish. She will feel so understood and loved if you embrace this as one of the critical ingredients of the date. In many cases, it is the whole point of the date for her, just as the sexual encounter is often the point for you.

## What Does It Mean to Pursue Your Wife?

*Finding Her Delightful Aspects*

Part of loving someone is pursuing them. Minimally, pursuing communicates, "I want to discover another delightful thing in you." To fall out of love with someone is to say, "I find nothing in you anymore that I take delight in," or "Your characteristics that repulse me are so great I cannot focus on the delightful aspects."

Your wife has many delightful aspects to her mind, emotions, spirit, and body. Too often, men only concentrate on the delightful aspects of a woman's body. But your wife needs to know you are interested in getting to know all the aspects of her by taking the time to explore these. Do not be in a hurry to rush to another area. Do not feel pressure to constantly find pleasure only in one aspect, such as sex. Enjoy all the delightful parts of who she is. Linger over her opinions, her creativity, her connection to God, her deep emotions about animals, the afflicted, and so forth.

God has many ways of keeping you delighted in your wife. You have probably found a number of them, and you just need to go back and drink them in to the fullest. Some men can get into a rut (dinner, a movie, sex) very easily and miss many things about their wives that are truly amazing and delightful. Make sure you regularly explore all the delightful aspects of your wife.

## Growth Exercises—Find Out All the Interesting Things about Her

Explore these areas about your wife and try to find out something new about her. What do you find delightful about her?

- Her interest in...
- Her ability to do...
- Her friendship with...
- Her work life...
- Her connection with God in regards to...
- Her teen years...
- Her elementary years...
- Her interest in changing the world in some arena...
- Her likes or dislikes of particular celebrities or politicians...
- Her ideas of the kids' future...
- Her growth goals...
- Her dream job...
- Her vacation dreams...

*Eliminating Competing Interests*

Pursuing your wife also means eliminating lawless and wickedly delightful activities that compete with her for your attention. When you allow something illegal or wicked to come into your life, it will distract from the attention you should pay to God and your wife. Only when you are willing to eliminate these pleasures will you be able to concentrate on her enough to find the new, delightful aspects of her personality you did not know before.

There are some delights that are not wrong, but they can nevertheless become an obsession that diverts your attention. These types of interests destroy the spirit of marriage and ultimately rob you of the companionship you sought when you began the marriage. These are the activities that you may not be able to moderate on your own and a wife becomes a window to hunting, football, baseball, gaming, and so on. Anything that becomes obsessive to the point where your wife notices or is concerned needs to be moderated or eliminated altogether.

## Growth Exercises—What Is Competing for Your Attention?

What things do your wife think you are obsessed with that are competing for your attention?

- Hobby...
- Work...
- Friends...
- Money...
- Computer...
- Video games...
- Sports...

*Drawing Her Out More*

You can constantly be on a search for new aspects and components that delight your wife. Expose her to new experiences, new places, and new thoughts so that you can watch her react, grapple, and interact with them. This will bring out delightful parts of her personality that you would never have known. There will be times when she expresses a strong conviction that you were unaware of because it never came up. You will see new fears and old memories she would never have shared if you had left her in the same old rut. Ask her about things she has always wanted to try that she has not attempted yet. Ask her about places she has always wanted to go and visit. Ask her to join you for some hobby. All these and many other ways allow you to mine the depths of your wife. She really is a gold mine of thoughts, feelings, desires, and gifts. Discover more of these and you will fall more in love with her.

### Growth Exercises—What Are Some Things You Could Introduce Her to?

Name fifteen new situations or activities that you could introduce your wife to that might uncover more delightful aspects about her.

*Focusing on What Is Mutually Enjoyable*

You can draw your wife into things you both enjoy. She does not need to be made to sit while you do your thing. She needs to be involved in something you can enjoy together. While there are activities you enjoy and would be totally happy if that was all you did, that type of selfishness does not help your marriage. Look for new activities that maybe neither of you have ever done. When she notices you suggest activities that could be mutually enjoyable or have a newness or freshness about them, she will love you all the more. For a list of possible new ideas to try as a couple, see **Appendix 4.**

### Growth Exercises—Commit to New Activities Together

From the list of ideas in Appendix 4, select ten to fifteen activities you both might enjoy and commit to trying them over the next weeks and months.

## Offer Her Hope for a Better Future

Another need a woman has is to see that the future can be brighter than the present. A function of romance is the possibility to experience a better future, even if the change or the experience is only for a few hours.

If a woman's world is reduced to the same monotony all the time, she loses hope and seeks escape. The husband's job is to provide this escape through romantic events and activities. This could mean that you treat her better during these times. Or that you give her more of your time.

The "better" future must be defined based on what she thinks is better, not your version. Many women would like proof that their whole life will not be full of rushing, kids, and insensitivity. This proof comes in your manners when there is no rush or kids. Do you treat her with the dignity and class she deserves, or do you just continue to throw verbal jabs or act in an insensitive manner? These add up to either giving your wife hope for a better future or painting the future with black, depressing darkness. It is up to you. Which will it be?

If you take her out but still treat her in the same rude and insensitive manner, then it is not really romance. Romance means that one is on their best behavior, that there is some type of change suggesting that things will get better.

Your wife may love to go to places and events that are fancy to her. She needs to see that the two of you are making upward progress, which is hopeful for her. This need can be met in several ways. It could be wearing fancy attire. It could be going to a nicer restaurant. It could mean going to an elegant event. There are several things your wife is interested in that would tell her there is hope for the future.

## Growth Exercises—How Can You Give Her Some Hope for a Better Future?

1. What events, activities, or gatherings would your wife like to go to that could give her hope for the future?

2. What are the various manners your wife wants to make your time together a romantic time? The following are examples and should not be taken as an exhaustive list:

   - Opening the door
   - Offering her your arm
   - Letting her go through the door first
   - Never leaving her side
   - Using "Please," "May I," "Excuse me," and "Thank you"
   - Ordering for her to show you know her tastes, style, and preferences
   - Not reading the paper or looking at your phone
   - Asking her a series of questions (see Gottman Card Deck app)
   - Having a prepared list of topics to discuss
   - Arranging for the babysitter yourself
   - Asking her to a predetermined place by Wednesday for a Friday outing
   - Roses or opening a gift
   - Getting dressed up
   - Various attentive mannerisms

# 20.

## MEETING HER PHYSICAL NEED:
## NONSEXUAL, TENDER TOUCH

Robert was a wonderful husband and father in almost all areas, but his wife, Blair, was emotionally living in a desert land. For ten years, she had put up with his utilitarian sexual demands, but inside she was dying. Blair's marriage was in trouble, and she could feel it. Rob did not know anything was wrong, that Blair was falling out of love with him.

Some of Blair's deepest emotional needs were left thirsting and barren while he pleased himself. She knew that it would quickly escalate into a sexual encounter if he touched her. "He never touches me unless he wants it to go to the bedroom," was her comment. What Rob did not realize was that he was killing the very thing he wanted most: a faithful and devoted companion for life. Through his lack of romance and tenderness, he was sabotaging his own goals for marriage.

A woman needs tender touch as much or more than a man wants or needs sex. She longs to be treated with tenderness and care. The man who understands his wife's need for hugs, caresses, and light touches is the man who will enjoy a rich relationship with his wife. Are you willing to go slowly and tenderly into the physical arena to minister to her? I would bet that if you were to meet the four nurturing needs we talk about in this section of the book, she would minister to you in the sexual department. It is hard for men to understand that as they brush past the tenderness to get to climax, they miss an opportunity for so much more. A man who understands his wife's need for tenderness throughout the marriage develops a woman who is much more receptive and alluring.

Much of the joy of tenderness is lost in our day and age of blatant sexuality. Husbands and wives need to take time for cuddling, spooning, hugging, nonsexual touching, and slow, easy, romantic touching. Too often, there is a rush to sexual fulfillment. While there is nothing wrong with sexual passion in marriage, there is a need to enjoy the journey rather than just speeding to the final destination. God has designed the woman so that she responds and needs much more than just sexual release. She needs to be treated with dignity and tenderness.

I have conducted what I call "hugging seminars" for married couples for years. I am amazed at how uncomfortable men are with hugging their wives. They often look like they are wrestling a bear. Most men do not know how to sustain a hug. Most wives have learned that if a hug is sustained for any length of time, their husbands' hands will go searching for sexual pleasure. Hugging seminars include a demonstration to men on how to hug their wives for five minutes without moving to sexual touch. It is usually important to have men put their hands around their wives and let their wives tell them what types of strokes they like. It is also essential for their wives to tell them what becomes sexual touch.

During these hugging seminars, many women have reported that when their husbands' hands are on their back, it is nonsexual touch. His hands placed on her sides convey sexual touch. Using the palm is most often nonsexual touch and the fingertips are more indicative of sexual touch.

Whoever said that people need five hugs a day was probably a woman. Most men don't need or even want any hugs on a given day, but women are much more able to receive this show of care and tenderness. To learn how to conduct your own hugging seminar, see **Appendix 5**.

## What Is Tender Touch to Your Wife?

*It May Be Romantic but Not Sexual*

In our marriage conferences, seminars, and workshops, Dana and I have heard many women say, "Men do not know how to touch in a nonsexual manner. They don't know how to stop before they get into sexual touch. They do not know the difference between sexual and nonsexual touch." Many women feel that men do not have the self-control to stop with nonsexual touch. Men don't realize that too much of this threatens a woman's security and may even crush her spirit. It can make her wary and even avoid his touch because she knows the touching means he wants more.

## It Is Specific to Your Wife

Each woman has specific ways she wants to receive tender touch. Ask your wife to help you find how she wants to be touched in a loving, tender, nonsexual way. The following are some examples to get you started.

- Neck massage
- Backrub
- Foot massage
- Brushing hair

## It Is an Energizer

Tender touch is one of the fastest ways to reenergize a person who is down or depressed. A sustained embrace will physically and emotionally energize a wife who is depressed, worried, or down about something. As a practical project, hug your wife for two minutes to comfort her.

## It Is a Means of Communication

When you touch your wife tenderly, it speaks volumes. You can communicate care, encouragement, support, healing, love, mercy, and trust. Your wife will hear things in your touch that you could never say aloud. She will begin a new level of trust in you as you speak to her soul through consistent, tender touch.

When you are away from each other, as bizarre as it sounds, you can communicate tender touch through the words you use to describe how you would touch your wife. Your wife needs to know that you would hug her if you were there. She may also gain great strength from your description of a hug. The next time you call your wife, give her a verbal hug.

## Growth Exercises—Communicate through Touch

Try and communicate the following messages just through touch. Keep trying until your wife agrees that a particular way of touching her communicates this particular message.

- Care
- Encouragement
- Trust
- Love
- Mercy
- Support
- Healing
- Forgiveness
- Confession
- Strength

## Tenderness During Sex

Many men are like impatient people on a train who always wonder when they will get to the final stop. When they get to the final train depot of life, they will realize that life's journey is more important than the ultimate destination. God wants us to show love in this world more than build up great treasures or power or accomplishments. The same is true of the sexual experience with your wife. Many men have only experienced rushed sexual release, which is how they continue to operate.

For your marriage to experience a greater level of intimacy, there must not be a selfish push for personal pleasure. It would help if you discovered the joys of pleasing your wife. You also need to learn to enjoy the whole of the sexual experience, which includes how to talk to your wife during an extended period of sexual tension and excitement.

### Lengthy Foreplay

One of the most common problems in marriages regarding sex is premature ejaculation. The man is unwilling to wait for his sexual desires to be climaxed, and the woman is mainly uninvolved and unfulfilled. You should be prepared to spend considerable time warming your wife up to the romantic and sexual experience. This means you must be ready to spend thirty minutes to four hours in a state of sexual tension and excitement. If you are not prepared to contain yourself for that length of time, you will rob your marriage of the greatest levels of intimacy and excitement.

Many women consider holding hands a part of foreplay. Men often need to expand what they see as the process of getting ready for sexual intimacy, but it is not just about the part in the bedroom. It's about how you treat her during the day and sometimes the whole week and month before.

It would help if you learned to control yourself to focus on pleasing and pleasuring your wife. If you make it your joy to see your wife pleased, your sexual experience will be enhanced. Selfish lovemaking is a very shortsighted experience.

There are several good books, both Christian and non-Christian, that walk a couple through how to solve the problem of premature ejaculation. I want to deal with the mindset resulting from this problem that damages intimacy.

After having been involved in marriage counseling for years and reading much of the literature designed to help couples in the sexual arena, I realized that most sexual encounters between a husband and a wife last no longer than ten minutes from the first contact to the clean-up. This is a tragic waste of time. This usually means that the husband has pleased himself, but his wife has been left feeling like a prostitute.

## Please Your Wife First

Prepare to please your wife and meet her needs in the sexual experience. Most women report that they would like the foreplay portion of a sexual encounter to last anywhere from half a day to two full days. Shopping, talking, and tenderness—well before any clothing is removed—can and should be treated as foreplay. This does not discount times for "quickies" from time to time, but if all a couple has is "quickies," where is the sharing, where is the intimacy?

A husband who seeks to meet his wife's needs approaches sexuality differently than a man who is consumed with pleasing himself. A godly husband is tender and interested in his wife and her needs, pleasure, and person. He directs himself to bring her to a place of desire and sexual excitement. Many sensitive men have suggested that they seek to get their wives to climax before they attempt to bring themselves to the final stages.

## Control the Timing of Your Release

The key in the sexual arena for the husband who wants to develop greater intimacy is to become sensitive to his wife in these moments. Men need to be disciplined and practice being able to hold an erection for between thirty minutes and two hours. Remember that often a woman is not as easily sexually aroused as a man and takes longer to become aroused. A sensitive husband will be prepared with tenderness and perhaps some lubricants for his wife. As he gently encourages her to relax into the sexual experience, she will be enabled to do so via thoughtful preparation.

In her interesting book *31 Days to Great Sex*, Sheila Wray Gregoire notes that men have sex to feel accepted, and women have sex because they are accepted.[15] When a man can demonstrate that he is more interested in pleasing and encouraging his wife in the sexual encounter, she will be more able to open up to the whole experience. A tender and selfless husband will have more joy in sex than a selfish man. Sex is another area where a man can display his love for his wife. When she feels your heart is to encourage and minister to her, she will give you more pleasure than you thought possible.

## Growth Exercises—Having a Talk about Sex

Discuss with your wife the following sensitive subjects:

- How long does it take her to get in the mood, ideally?
- How would she prefer the sexual experience to begin?
- What are the various positions she has been interested in trying?
- What does she want to talk about during sex?
- What brings her to a climax?
- What is a major turn-off in sexual relations?
- What are distractions to full enjoyment of sexual pleasure?
- Does she experience pain during normal sexual encounters?
- Are there any reasons she is having difficulties with sexual relations?

The above discussion points are not designed to be a full discussion of the sex within marriage. There are very good books that will help a married couple work through the various issues of making love. Unfortunately, there are a number of books about sex that give license to immorality and sin. These books should not form the basis of your knowledge or direction in the sexual area. Remember, as godly husbands, our call is to keep godliness in mind at all times.

## Temperament and Your Wife's Sexual Mood

Most women are under tremendous pressure in many areas of their lives, and sex is often just one more duty to go along with the kids, house, work, laundry, meals, and so forth. Many women have a hard time concentrating on sexual excitement when children are in the next room. It takes time and variety to move a woman to interest in this area. A sensitive husband realizes that his wife needs time away from these pressures to connect with her romantic and sexual self. He also realizes that his wife is often more interested in pleasing him than being aroused. He would be wise not to demand a sexual dynamo each time.

It can be helpful for a godly husband to bring his understanding of his wife into his planning for a sexual encounter. Each woman is different, but her personality and temperament traits have a significant bearing on sexual relations. Let me give you a few examples.

If your wife is a playful and fun-loving person, she is the most naturally sexually interested but wants an atmosphere of fun and play in the bedroom. She tends to be silly and not serious. She responds better to a fun atmosphere than to a dark, mysterious encounter. If the sexual encounter can be preceded by what she considers fun, she will carry that into the sexual encounter.

If your wife likes to be in charge in every aspect of her life, she will respond the most strongly when she is more in control of the direction and timing of the sexual encounter. She is not interested in always being on the bottom in sexual encounters. She is also most interested in getting to the goal and may tend to push past the important arousal period to get this accomplished so she can get on to other things.

If your wife is amiable and artistic, she is most willing to engage in sexual episodes because her husband needs it. However, she is most interested in having relations with her friend, not someone she has just argued with. She is also directed to notice the setting of the encounter. She is less inclined to fully embrace her sexuality in a dumpy or unappealing environment.

If your wife is precise, analytic, and subjective, she is more prone to notice the mood of the evening or the encounter. She responds more easily if things are perfect and planned. She does not usually regard surprises as a good thing. She tends to be shy and may prefer the encounter in the dark. She may be interested in interacting with a deep, intellectual topic before, during, or after the encounter. Her mind must be involved.

It would be helpful to bring your understanding of your wife's temperament and personality into your thinking about sexual relations. If you go to all the work of really loving her—not just focusing on sex itself—it will pay rich dividends in your marriage and your life.

One important thing to remember is that all of the aspects of nurture that have been discussed in this chapter are means of foreplay for your wife. Think of your wife's sexual ability as the glow plug in a diesel motor. It will not fire off until properly warmed up and glowing. The goal of a husband who wants a good marriage and great sex is to keep his wife constantly glowing by submitting to the processes outlined above.

# PRINCIPLE #7—DEFENDER

"Remember the Lord who is great and awesome,
and fight for your brothers,
your sons, your daughters,
your wives and your houses."

Nehemiah 4:14 NASB

—◦◦◦—

**Jeff allowed his wife, Irene, to do whatever** she wanted even though both admitted that what she regularly wanted often put her in situations to get drunk and cheat on him. After years of a "boring marriage," as she called it, Irene found a group of ladies at work who liked to party and have a "good time." They introduced her to a whole new world of alcohol, drugs, men, late nights, and adult fun. She enjoyed the party life more than the boring life at home with her husband and children. She was still young. She was constantly told she should use her beauty for fun before she was too old to enjoy it.

Within a year and a half of this adult lifestyle, Irene's husband and family were no longer good enough for her. She sued for divorce because her husband would not enter into her fun wholeheartedly. He was no good. He had tried to be good to her by letting her do what she wanted, but it resulted in disaster. I remember speaking with Irene before the divorce became final, and Jeff was still willing to take her back. I told her that her path would leave her diseased, used, beaten, and old before her time. She could change her mind, and Jeff would take her back, but she rejected her husband and my prediction.

Following the divorce, she leaned into the bar scene for about three years, dating a various assortment of immoral men and destroying the emotional stability of her small children. After almost five years of party life, she concluded that her old, boring, no-good husband was better than she thought. She wanted the love of her girls. There was, however, no repairing the damage that her immoral freedom had cost. He did not want her back, and he had the kids. Only then did she understand the consequences of what she had done. My prediction had come true in only five years. Irene was diseased, beaten, old, and alone.

Unfortunately, this scene is being played out in homes everywhere. Yet, it is the man's fault as much, if not more, than the wife. As Irene's husband, Jeff's part in this calamity was that he needed to find a way to protect her before all of this started. He needed to protect her from the friends who had seduced her into this soul-sucking, marriage-destroying lifestyle. I have worked with husbands who were able to protect their wives from these lies and destructive activities, but they started much earlier with the cooperation of their wives. It is important to protect your wife from the threats that can destroy her when she still wants to be protected.

## Defending Your Wife and Family

One of the jobs of being a godly husband is knowing your wife well enough to defend her from that which would destroy her. None of us can handle perfect, unlimited freedom. All healthy relationships have boundaries and limits. When a husband lovingly and tenderly but firmly defends his wife from that which would destroy her, he saves everyone from untold heartache.

It is possible for a husband to be overbearing, harsh, and selfish in his role of defender. Don't do that! These approaches are wrong and counterproductive. The husband must love his wife and work with her to protect her, just as he must let her help him keep away from things that will destroy him. We all know that we are drawn toward things that are bad for us; it's the sinful nature within all of us. Ask your wife how you can help her be the best she can be. You are trying to be helpful where she wants the help, not controlling. You want her to be drawn to your love, care, and concern, not repelled by your attempts to control and dominate.

This area of defense is a neglected discussion in marriage counseling today because people believe that the other person must have total freedom. This is never the case in any relationship. All relationships have limits. I cannot have a relationship with my children if I never limit my evenings out so that I can be with them. I cannot have friendships with other people if I do not limit my comments about their weaknesses and areas of incompetency. I cannot have a relationship with God unless

I restrict my behavior to not offend Him with every action I take. Marriage is no different. If two people are going to stay in a marriage relationship, there are some things they cannot do. You could do them if you were single. You could do them if you don't care about this relationship. But if you care and want your marriage to be good, there must be some limits on you and her.

Many men want to be the protector of their wives but only in physical terms. They are ready to protect her from a robber or rogue animal, but those things don't happen that often. A husband's understanding of how he needs to protect his wife needs to grow out of the real threats in our current culture. Protect her from what stresses her out. Protect her from what is toxic to her personality. Protect her from people who exhaust her. Protect her from overwork and hyper-scheduling. Let her know that you love her and don't expect her to be Superwoman. You need to protect her from threats in her real life.

What do some of these restrictions look like? Some are particular to that person (neatness, frugality, punctuality, and so on). Some are moral restrictions (no adultery, stealing, or lying). Some are addictive issues (porn, alcohol, drugs, football, credit cards), and some are uniquely personal (no scary movies, no practical jokes, no animals, the children, no night driving, and so on). Find out what your wife needs to be protected from and protect her. Don't try and protect her from things she doesn't want to be protected from. Just as God waits for us to invite Him into our lives to empower us, so husbands should not barge in and tell our wives what we think they are doing wrong or what we think they need protecting from.

The point is that every relationship has restrictions on both people. Some you impose upon yourself to stay in the relationship, some the other person imposes upon you. Some are necessary to keep from destroying yourself, and some are mutually agreed upon that are particular to that relationship. She does not want you to become her accuser or jailer. It would be best to accept the responsibility of lovingly defending your wife against others, herself, her desires, and her fears. This is not an easy job because it keeps changing as she grows and ages. The type of defense she needed at twenty-five is not what she needs at forty-five or sixty-five. Your wife is expecting you to be her defender.

## Where does your wife need your protection?

This last chapter covers seven arenas where your wife needs protection in the spiritual, mental, emotional, physical, and financial realms.

Chapter 21—Defending Your Wife in Seven Key Arenas

# 21.

## DEFENDING YOUR WIFE IN
## SEVEN KEY ARENAS

---

This final chapter will go over seven arenas to defend your wife. Keep in mind that she must be able to defend and restrict you in some of these arenas as well.

### Arena 1—Physical

Your wife needs you to defend her in the physical arena in several ways. The following is just a partial list of topics. Discuss each area with your wife, and then ask her if there are other physical issues she may need your defense, protection, or restriction. Ask her if there are physical dangers or concerns she would like you to protect her from.

#### Safety

Your wife needs to feel as though she is safe from attack. Whatever it takes for her to get this type of security, do it. This could include locks, a security system, a front door camera, a different neighborhood, having guns in the home (or not), and so forth. Another example would be to make sure she is safe coming out of a public function late at night. Or making sure her car has safe tires and is running well, so she won't break down on the side of the road. Remember, it doesn't matter if you feel safe; it matters if *she* feels safe.

## Help

Your wife needs to know who, how, when, and where she can contact help in certain dangerous situations. Show her what numbers to call if she gets a flat tire or is in an accident and can't reach you. Some women need help lifting objects that are too heavy for them. Some need protection from unscrupulous businesses trying to take advantage of them. In this day and age, they need to know how to identify and avoid internet scams and security risks to protect their identities and the family. What are some of the areas where your wife needs help?

## Procedures

Your wife needs to know how to do things like changing a tire, jump-starting her car, filling her gas tank, how to drive defensively, or how to drive in snow. Other procedures could be knowing where the fire extinguisher is and how it works, what to do when the breaker trips or when the electricity goes off. These are all things that could help her feel safer.

## Abilities

Your wife needs to know the basics of street survival. More and more women are interested in feeling they personally have the ability to fend off an attacker. This makes them feel safer. She needs to sense that she knows what to do if she is in a tense, disturbing, or violent situation. Many women do not want to practice what to do if a car-jacking or rape happens to them. This is where the loving, persistent practice is necessary. They have to be ready. Sometimes having her go to a class is better than teaching her yourself. These could teach her self-defense, karate, mace training, pepper training, learning how to handle a gun, or screaming, shouting, and kicking.

## Arena 2—Addictions

Your wife may be subject to overindulging in certain areas. If this is the case, one of your responsibilities is to help her stop or see the need for help. You should not just let her be exposed to the full force of her temptations. They may destroy her. Be sensitive to your wife's needs in this area, and do not give in to her desires just because she wants them. You cannot re-parent her, but she does need you to help her.

## Food

Many women struggle with their weight—with no help from their husbands. In fact, men are often sarcastic about this area. Your sarcasm about her weight or how much she is eating will not help. Find out what would help her. Many women need to be accepted for who they are, and only that will give them the energy and ability to tackle an issue like overeating. If she tends to overeat or like chocolate or ice cream too much, then help her by defending her from her desires. Watch for signs of bulimia, anorexia, or other symptoms indicating that your wife may be influenced by some type of compulsive or addictive behavior.

### Drink

Some women can develop an addiction to alcohol, soft drinks, or some other beverage. Some women become dependent on a glass of wine or a beer every day. If it is a problem for her or both of you, then work with her to stop. If there is the possibility of overdrinking, it is important to educate yourself on various ways to help. The first way to help that comes to your mind may not work. Find solutions that actually work from those who know how to help people with these problems.

### Drugs

Some people can be extremely tempted by illegal or prescription drugs. If your wife has a tendency or a history of problems in these areas or sees it becoming a problem, the earlier you step in, the better. These types of issues will destroy your family. Many husbands do not step in until their wives are already hooked. This is often too late. Again let me suggest that a godly husband cares enough to talk with drug addiction experts on what they can do to love their spouse through this issue.

## Arena 3—Mental

Your wife needs to know that you are prepared to step in and keep her from seeing or thinking about ideas, images, or situations that are too strong or disturbing to her. The following is only a partial list of these. Ask your wife to share other things in this arena where she needs you to step in and help her.

### Her past

Some women have had difficult, even horrific, things happen to them in their past. They are often at the mercy of those images or feelings that wash over them. They need your help in understanding what is going on and being a support and encouragement toward a solution. So many women need to feel that their husbands are allies and not a source of condemnation. Just as when a bone breaks and heals stronger in the place of the break, a wife's past may become a place of great strength if she is allowed to heal.

## Friends

Some of your wife's friends can be in such horrible situations that your wife cannot mentally remove herself. You may have to help that friend or get your wife away from that situation. Your wife may also need protection from friends who expose her to situations that draw her heart out in a way that will wound her or tempt her. I cannot stress this protection from stressful, immoral, or toxic friends enough. Help your wife find and keep good friends. Do all you reasonably can to help her stay away from and sort through bad friends.

## Television

Be aware that a number of reality-based TV shows plant images of rape and violence and other unsafe behaviors, which may well cause your wife to feel unsafe. There may be shows your wife enjoys watching but portray images, ideas, or situations she cannot handle or get away from. It is your job to change the channel, even over your wife's objections, just as she would change the channel on a show full of naked ladies. Some of these shows can make it seem like these bizarre things happen to people all the time, but in reality, they are extremely rare.

## Movies

Be aware that many women tend to be more upset by violence than men. The images can deeply disturb them and make them feel unsafe. It does not matter whether you can handle it; it matters whether she can handle it. Do not take your wife to a movie that will disturb her for days or months. There are movies that you simply should not watch. Just because you love violent movies does not mean she can handle them. If your wife is disturbed by the images and storylines in the movies that you watch, then don't watch them with her.

## Books

There are an increasing number of books that graphically detail affairs and sexual situations. If your wife reads these types of books, you might want to watch her reactions in the days and weeks after she reads them. If after she reads a particular kind of book or magazine, she is more dissatisfied with your marriage, family, or herself, you might want to discuss with her whether this is a helpful pursuit.

## Internet and Social Media

Too many women (and men) spend a large chunk of their time, money, and energy searching and shopping on the internet or scrolling through their social media platforms without end. While these mediums aren't bad things, they can become a problem if your wife starts comparing her life to what appears to be the best of other people's lives. Or if she can't control her shopping habits or engages with old high school or college boyfriends or the back-and-forth volley of contention and conflict from comments. Watch for signs of secrecy, anxiety, discontentment, and multiple shipping boxes on your doorstep. These might be signs of your wife needing protection in these areas.

## Arena 4—Relational

Your wife has and needs a number of relationships. Some of the relationships could be very draining to her. On the other hand, some are very helpful and encouraging. Some of her relationships may present various temptations. It is your job to know how to protect your wife, encourage her, and know when to suggest eliminating a friendship before it becomes a danger to your marriage. Which of her friends, work colleagues, or neighbors wear her out and leave her drained? Is there some way you could step in and rescue her from being drained by that person?

### Her friends

Many women develop friendships with other women or men who are unhealthy. It is important that you begin the process early of evaluating her friendships (and she should evaluate yours) to see whether these could be heading in the wrong direction. Help her develop friendships with positive people who affirm her best qualities, keep her grounded in her faith, and seek God's best. If a friendship is allowed to deepen with a wicked person, then it will be virtually impossible to keep the flow of wicked ideas away from your family.

### Your friends

There may be people you have been with or are developing a friendship with that leave your wife scared, threatened, nervous, tempted, or emotionally attacked. These friends of yours need to be limited or eliminated. You are the defender of your wife's soul. She comes first. Do not put up with a friend who makes a pass at your wife. Do not put up with a friend who makes your wife feel physically or emotionally unsafe. And do not make friends with other women, including neighbors or coworkers, without your wife's knowledge, involvement, and consent.

## Children

Many women feel they are not as special in their husband's eyes as their children or the children from a previous marriage. If this type of rivalry starts, it can destroy your family. Your wife needs to be secure in her place as number one. You need to defend your love for your wife in the face of your children's request and special privileges. If you allow your children to appear to come before your wife, ground is lost in the relationship. In a godly home, God is first, then your spouse, then your children. Things get messed up when the priority order gets switched around.

## Arena 5—Emotional

Your wife needs to be confident that she can reveal her emotions to you, and you will understand and defend her. In a sense, you want her to be able to trust you with her deepest secrets. She needs to know that you will never use this information against her. You must not allow her to be regularly backed into an emotional corner or to get beat on emotionally. You must defend her.

### Anger

Most wives cannot take their husband's anger, even when it is not directed at them. It seems odd to suggest that you must defend your wife from your own anger, but that is exactly what you must do. It is also important not to let a boss or friend vent anger consistently at your wife. You need to defend her in this. Most anger is just a selfishness problem, and if we were to work on it, everyone would get a blessing.

### Verbal abuse, gestures, and name-calling

These are childish ways to get our way and result in a wife who cannot trust us. Yes, they may be used to win a marital argument, but you will damage the relationship in the process. Step up and fight fair. Have honest discussions and be willing to be wrong. Losing an argument is better than shaming her with verbal abuse, gestures, and name-calling.

### Sarcasm, teasing

Women know that teasing and sarcasm are often a way of saying the truth or a belief, granting ourselves the ability to back out by saying, "I was only kidding." These forms of communication usually make a woman feel insecure. Your words will have more impact if they are not wrapped in sarcasm. Too many men use sarcasm as their primary means of communication and wonder why their wife doesn't listen. Speak clearly and openly.

## Crying

Every so often, women need to vent their feeling and emotions by crying physically. Your wife must have the ability to cry in a secure environment. Be there to comfort and console her, usually by just holding her and being there. Never tell a woman to "stop crying!" It is offensive to her, and she will resent you for it.

## Arena 6—Financial

Under the topic of security, we discussed a wife's deep need to be financially secure. Your wife needs you to build a financial wall of protection around her. This is not a financial prison but a place of safety and security in the economic arena. Many unscrupulous businesses and con artists target women thinking they are weak. This could be pyramid schemes, automotive companies, door-to-door salespeople, or even parties they attend to purchase makeup, kitchen tools, clothing, or home goods. Your job is to protect your wife from anyone trying to part her from her money.

### Debt

Women are generally much more sensitive to debt than men. Your wife likely wants a cash reserve and all bills paid. All people tend to buy on impulse, but men buy bigger. A godly husband finds a way to introduce a realistic budget to their marriage and family. If your budgeting style doesn't make sense to her, then find another way of conveying the ideas. Both of you need to be moving in the same direction on debt elimination.

### Sources of income

It can be beneficial to understand your wife's expectations toward the income for the family. Some women resist being put into a place where they are the primary source of income for the family. This is not true for all women. Some thrive on it. How do you and she understand where the family income will come from? It is clear from Proverbs 31 that it is biblical for women to generate lots of income for their family, so don't be surprised when she wants a part in this too.

### Unwise ventures

Men hear and think up all types of ridiculous schemes they think will make them rich, famous, or happy. If you launch ahead without checking with your wife, you'll miss out on her valuable insight and internal warning bells. Also, engaging in risky ventures can cause her to become insecure and worried.

## Arena 7—Organizational

You must understand your wife enough to build the organizational protection and safety she needs in your family. There will be times when your wife needs you to take the heat, to be the "point position" for the family. At times, she will need to use you to protect herself from those who would trouble your family.

### Headship

Headship means taking responsibility and searching for wisdom. Are you the person who checks all the possibilities and is open to all options? This is what makes you a wise man and the head of the home. If you are unwilling to consider any other options other than your own, you are foolish and not wise. Many men destroy their wife's security by transferring blame to her if anything goes wrong. If you tell your wife, "Okay, but if I get in trouble, it's your fault," this makes her the head of the family, always making her insecure. If you tell her after a failure, "Why did you let me do that?" or "Why didn't you stop me? It's your fault," then you've just transferred headship to her by placing the responsibility on her.

### Work

Many women have jobs outside of the home. (Hopefully, her first job will be at home as a wife and mother during the child-rearing years.) If she works outside of the house, you need to establish a relationship with her boss. If the relationship constantly changes or the boss outranks the husband regarding importance, this will usually produce insecurity.

### Growth Exercises—How Will You Protect Your Wife?

Discuss each arena with your wife and ask her if there are other issues where you could defend, protect, or restrict for her good and the good of the family.

- Where does she feel unsafe?
- What could you put in place to help her feel more secure?
- What procedures, abilities, or information do you need to expose her to, teach her, or practice with her?
- Where are the areas she needs to defend, protect, or restrict you for your good and the good of the family?
- What can she do to help you?

# CONCLUSION

The present culture no longer allows a husband to coast along in his relationship with his wife because she may not be financially dependent upon him. He must begin to be a husband in the described biblical terms covered in this book, or his wife may take the world's approach to relationships and leave.

It is time for men to fulfill their God-given duty and love their wives as Christ loved the Church. Your wife should be a better person following her exposure to you, sharing her life's experiences with you. One day, each husband will be evaluated concerning the job he did on the number one project God gave him on this earth: marriage. By understanding her needs, you'll be one step closer to hearing, "Well done, good and faithful servant."

If I can learn these principles, then you can too. So many men listen to or read this material and tell me it is too much, that they could never do it. But that is not true. I am living proof that the biblical principles in this book are doable. The relationship that grows out of a man becoming a godly husband is amazing. I began the journey to learn how to truly love a wife when I was single with no marriage prospects. I had just had the fourth woman I was seriously dating tell me she would not marry me. I went to a conference where a speaker opened up the Scriptures, and I heard things I had never heard before about becoming a godly man and a godly husband. The speaker offered to mentor me in these completely different ways of treating a woman. It took me longer than most to change my ways, but it has paid rich dividends. It took me four-and-a-half years of practicing the principles in this book before God introduced me to my bride, Dana.

I strongly suggest that you read, re-read, and re-read this book, doing the exercises and practicing being biblical. I have watched how these principles transform marriages, individuals, and families. God's Word teamed up with God's Spirit inside a willing man is awesome.

If you have completed your first or fifteenth time through *Becoming a Godly Husband*, keep going. If you continue to grow in your ability to be a godly husband, you will have a fantastic marriage that is wholly pleasing to God. Not only that, but your wife will bask in the glow of your love. This is not the kind of book you read once and then move on. Reread it. Look up all the Scriptures. Start a small group of men who want to go through this material. I know of men who have been teaching a class on this material for fifteen-plus years. It has been truly life-changing for many guys.

Let me tell you a few of the things people have said to me when they or their husbands put these principles into practice.

"I wish you could have a husband like my husband," she bragged. Only five weeks earlier, this lady had told me that she was leaving her husband because of the horrible way he was treating her. I asked her to wait until her husband had gone through the first three lessons of the class for husbands. She agreed and watched her husband become a transformed man right before her eyes.

Another man came back to say thanks for the change that had taken place in his life. He was in love with his wife again, and she was in love with him. This couple acted like newlyweds. She giggled, and they turned to go out to their car arm in arm. I could see they were truly in love again.

A lady pulled me aside after a church service and, with tears, said, "I don't know what you have done to my husband, but keep going. Our marriage has never been this good. He is treating me unbelievably well. Thanks."

An older lady grabbed both of my hands after church one Sunday and told me through tears, "My husband is getting ready to retire, and I could not think of anything worse than more of my husband around the house. But then you invited him to this class, and he is completely changed. I can't wait till he retires, and I get this gentle, tender, and loving man all day long. Thank you. You have no idea how much this means to me."

I overheard one wife comment to her husband, "I have never seen you care for me like this before. Thanks, I really can see that you love me."

Yet another husband had tears in his eyes as he told me that he never had anything to say to his wife before taking this course. "It is a tragedy, isn't it?" he asked, "We used to sit in the car going someplace and have nothing to say to each other. Now I know how to enjoy my wife. Thank you."

The examples above are just a few quotes and stories about men who have become serious about loving their wives. Many men don't get motivated until their wife leaves. Some don't get interested until she threatens to sue them and take fifty percent of all they have built up over the years. Many men just want to have the kind of marriage they thought they would have when the whole thing started.

We have learned how to be a godly husband and to meet our wife's needs at the deepest levels. The list of actions we have memorized is not only for our benefit but for our wife, our marriage, our family, and the glory of Christ. Only when we begin to act like Christ will we fully embrace what marriage is supposed to be.

The ideas and concepts in this book are the keys to understanding why your wife acts, thinks, speaks, and reacts the way she does. I do not believe you will be able to find a situation you and your wife could go through where these principles would not apply. Your wife is counting on you to meet her needs.

If you are going to become a truly great and godly husband, you must commit these concepts to memory. Practice them repeatedly until they become the way you handle problems and situations with your wife. Remember that these ideas and principles do not come naturally, and you will slip back into your masculine way of handling your wife unless you work on these concepts. You are responsible for one hundred percent of the climate of your marriage, so memorize these ideas and be able to perform them in a natural way. It takes about three years of working on these principles before fully grasping how they impact your wife, so keep working on them. I recommend you go over these principles at least once a year.

Never forget or take for granted how the nature of your marriage has changed from just barely applying the concepts related in this book. If you persevere and treat your wife according to the dictates of Scripture in this book, you will enjoy a marriage that other men only dream of.

I hope you will share the secrets you've learned and mastered with other men. Explain them to another man so you can help him and refresh your memory simultaneously. What would the world look like if there were more godly marriages? More men stepping into their divine husband role? Never discount the impact one godly marriage can make, and it can start with yours.

Let us review the basic principles again:

# H. U. S. B. A. N. D

———⊶∞⊷———

## Honor:
treat her better than anyone else in your life

## Understanding:
be quick to apologize; know everything about her

## Security:
provide financial, emotional, mental, and physical security

## Building Unity:
never make her the enemy; do activities together

## Agreement:
work out a process of decision-making together

## Nurture:

SPIRIT: Leadership—lead her spirit to a better place

MENTAL: Communication—talk with her an hour every day

EMOTIONAL: Romance—date her every week

PHYSICAL: Tender touch—touch her in a positive, non-sexual way

## Defender:
protect her from what will derail or destroy her

# APPENDIX 1
# HOW ARE YOU DOING?
# NEEDS ASSESSMENT

How are you doing as a godly husband? This simple quiz will give you some insight into the problem areas and where to begin.

1.  Every day, I honor my wife by making her my number one priority next to God. I compliment her, eliminate disrespect towards her, and tell her I love her every day.

    Always        Often        Occasionally        Never

2.  I understand my wife is more sensitive than me in many areas. I show her that I understand this by apologizing when I have hurt her, being open to her help to become a better person, and knowing more about her personality, family patterns, leadership styles, love languages, and past baggage more than anyone else does.

    Always        Often        Occasionally        Never

3.  I make my wife feel secure: financially, relationally, emotionally, physically, and spiritually. She feels more secure with me in her life.

    Always        Often        Occasionally        Never

4.    I build unity and direction in my marriage and family by never letting her be the enemy, doing lots of positive and meaningful activities with her, directing our marriage toward a series of righteous goals, and accomplishing the goals as a team.

Always    Often    Occasionally    Never

5.    I promote agreement in our marriage instead of fighting by seeking wisdom, not my own way, by having a series of preset decisions, working through a decision-making process, and making room for her ideas.

Always    Often    Occasionally    Never

6.    I nurture my wife *mentally* by engaging in intimate, regular communication each day for about an hour; *emotionally* through weekly romance; *physically* by regularly touching her tenderly, and *spiritually* by leading her to God and a positive expression of her personality and helping her understand her conscience.

Always    Often    Occasionally    Never

7.    I defend my wife from toxic mental, verbal, physical, emotional, relational, and spiritual threats.

Always    Often    Occasionally    Never

Suppose you answered "always" and "often" to many of these questions, great job! It sounds like you are doing well at meeting many of your wife's needs, and you probably have a pretty good, if not great, marriage, but there are always more ways to improve. If you answered "occasionally" or "never," these areas could use some additional work. Don't worry. You can refocus your effort and time building these areas until you get to a place where you meet her needs.

This book will help you if you are willing to roll up your sleeves and do the hard work. It'll be the best work you've ever done.

# APPENDIX 2
# TEMPERAMENT STYLES

Temperament styles explain a lot about how we react or respond to situations in life. The following is a listing of basic temperament impulses. Each of us "sense" or "feel" these various impulses in our lives, but a few of these impulses tend to dominate, which we regularly act upon. Note which impulses you tend to act upon and which ones your wife tends to act upon. Note the differences you observe between them. When you are finished going through these, make a few observations about how each of you will usually act under the pressures of life, and what things will be very difficult for each of you to do.

| Temperament / Impulse | Husband | Wife |
|---|---|---|
| Talkative or Reserved? | | |
| Weak-willed or Strong-willed? | | |
| Angry or Happy? | | |
| Outgoing or Shy? | | |
| Stable or Unstable? | | |
| Determined or Hesitant? | | |
| Sarcastic or Polite? | | |
| Enthusiastic or Detached? | | |
| Disciplined or Undisciplined? | | |

| Temperament / Impulse | Husband | Wife |
|---|---|---|
| Independent or Dependent? | | |
| Domineering or Amenable? | | |
| Optimistic or Pessimistic? | | |
| Warm or Cold? | | |
| Content or Restless? | | |
| Considerate or Inconsiderate? | | |
| Personable or Impersonal? | | |
| Dependable or Undependable? | | |
| Practical or Extravagant? | | |
| Proud or Humble? | | |
| Friendly or Unfriendly? | | |
| Others Focused or Self Focused? | | |
| Productive or Unproductive? | | |
| Self-Sufficient or Needy? | | |
| Compassionate or Merciless? | | |
| Loud or Quiet? | | |
| Decisive or Indecisive? | | |
| Trustful or Distrustful | | |
| Emotional or Unemotional | | |
| Carefree or Burdened? | | |
| Leader or Follower? | | |
| Exaggerates or Understated | | |
| Conservative or Liberal? | | |
| Loyal or Disloyal? | | |

| Temperament / Impulse | Husband | Wife |
|---|---|---|
| Critical or Accepting? | | |
| Perfectionist or Compromising? | | |
| Analytical or Theoretical? | | |
| Spontaneous or Planner? | | |
| Confident or Fearful? | | |

## Husband Observations:

_____

_____

_____

_____

_____

_____

_____

_____

## Wife Observations:

_____

_____

_____

_____

_____

_____

_____

_____

# APPENDIX 3
# THE FIVE LOVE LANGUAGES

## Words of Encouragement

Those who prefer to give and receive love through this love language are those who give positive, encouraging, and uplifting words. They are the most reluctant to give a discouraging word. They also feel the most loved when others tell them in some form that their actions are helpful, good, or positive.

## Acts of Service

Those who prefer this form of love usually demonstrate their love by helping another person in some tangible way. They will automatically see the little things that need to be done which will be of a tremendous help to the other person. The fact that they are willing to do them is their way of saying "I love you," not that they enjoy doing the job. They also feel the most loved when people do things for them to relieve their load.

## Quality Time

Those who prefer this type of love are those who would like to have you enjoy special time with them. These people have favorite activities, and those they love always get invited. It is a sign of love to include certain people in on the special activity. They also receive love by being invited to spend special time with others.

They may not even like the activity, but the knowledge that it is special to the other person draws them to try it.

---

## Gift-Giving

Those who prefer this love language are those who enjoy giving gifts to special people. The fact that they give gifts (many times they are not expensive) to a person is a sign of love and care. They also prefer receiving gifts (usually lots) which tells them that you love them.

---

## Physical Touch and Closeness

The person who has this type of love language speaks and receives volumes through touch. They love to touch and to be touched. They are those who enjoy being close. This person communicates their love through touch and receives love through touch.

(Gary Chapman, www.5lovelanguages.com, used with permission)

# APPENDIX 4

# ACTIVITIES TO DO AS A COUPLE

| | | |
|---|---|---|
| Building things | Binge-watching a series | Board games |
| Crafts | Tennis | Playing/making music |
| Racing | Racquetball | Singing/karaoke |
| Working on cars | Golf | Hosting guests/parties |
| Sewing | Talking | Baking |
| Crochet | Waterskiing | Drawing |
| Cricket | Surfing | Building models |
| Volleyball | Watching baseball | Snorkeling |
| Football | Hiking | Scuba diving |
| Basketball | Working out | Rollerblades |
| Spear fishing | Karate | Roller hockey |
| Deep sea/fly fishing | Judo | Ice hockey |
| Swimming/sunbathing | Improvisational games | Ice skating |
| Downhill skiing | Learning something new | Camping |
| Cross-country skiing | Flying | Darts |
| Tubing/Tobogganing | Mountain biking | Frisbee golf |
| Snowmobiling | Road biking | Frisbee |
| Snowshoeing | Jogging | Archery |
| Motorcycles | Amusement parks | Flying ultra-light planes |
| ATV | Roller coasters | Sailing/boating |
| 4-wheeling | Pets | Nature walks |
| Reading | Pinball/arcade games | Flying RC Airplanes |
| Watching T.V./movies | Air hockey | Beach |

| | | |
|---|---|---|
| Beach games | Writing | Boxing |
| Horseback riding | Acting | Trying new restaurants |
| Going out to eat | Community projects | Weight lifting |
| Fishing | Disabled ministries | Shopping |
| Aerobics/exercise class | Planting special seeds | Used book shopping |
| Pottery | Audio books | Redecorating the house |
| Antiquing | Taking drives | Remodeling/updating |
| Boat shows | Painting | Yardwork/gardening |
| Home & Garden shows | Auto repair/detailing | Picnicking |
| RV shows/RVing | Whitewater rafting | Wine tasting/making |
| Bowling | Picnic games | Making new friends |
| Bike riding | Laser tag | Concerts |
| Hang gliding | Rock climbing | Symphony |
| Sky diving | Canoeing | Scooters |
| Museums | Kayaking | Jet skiing |
| Prof. sports tickets | Visiting historic sites | Learning a language |
| Cave spelunking | Conventions | Arcades |
| Mountain climbing | Retreats | Shuffleboard |
| Gardening | Speakers | Ping pong |
| Woodworking | Backpacking | Windsurfing |
| Birdwatching | Triathlon | Collecting things |
| Traveling | Marathons | Video games |
| Photography | Soccer | Serving together |
| Developing pictures | Quilting | Self-defense class |
| Cooking together | Embroidery | Ballets |
| Ballroom dancing/classes | Bow hunting | Coffee shops |
| Going dancing | Rifle hunting | Jewelry making |
| Doing puzzles | Investing | Paddle boarding |
| Card games | Calligraphy | Dinner parties |
| Going to plays | Video games | Beach volleyball |
| Art galleries | Running a 5/10K | Exploring |
| Yoga | Softball | Taking walks |
| Pottery | Water parks | Opera |
| Flying kites | Horseshoes | Window shopping |
| Mountain climbing | Getting pedicures | Creating art |

# APPENDIX 5
## CONDUCT YOUR OWN
## HUGGING SEMINAR

---

Find out what types of nonsexual touch your wife likes.

When does she need you to hold her?

How does she want you to hug her from the back, side, front?

What types of hugs are sexual and which ones are nonsexual?

Does your wife enjoy holding hands?

In what situations does your wife enjoy your arm around her?

What is your wife's definition of cuddling?

When does she just want you near her?

What ways do you touch her that she does not appreciate?

What are ways that she would like you to touch her?

When you are out in public, what type of touch does she like?

How would she like to sit at restaurants?

How can you touch her without it ending in the bedroom?

What are the three most meaningful types of nonsexual touches?

# NOTES

1   http://famousquotefrom.com/benjamin-disraeli/

2   For more about this, I outline thirty-one ways to bring correction into your kids' lives in my book, *Wise Parenting: Creating the Joy of Family.*

3   For more on this, please reference the wonderful book, *The Five Love Languages* by Gary Chapman.

4   Chapman, Gary D., *The 5 Love Languages: The Secret to Love that Lasts* (Chicago: Northfield Publishing, 2015).

5   "Loving with all your...brain," February 15, 2007, CNN Medical Correspondents, Elizabeth Cohen and Amy Burkholder, Male and Female Brain Studies, https://www.cnn.com/2007/HEALTH/02/14/love.science/.

6   Patterson, Kerry; Grenny, Joseph; McMillan, Ron; Switzler, Al, *Crucial Conversations, Second Edition* (New York: McGraw-Hill Publications, 2012), 117–18.

7   Shawchuck, Norman and Robert Moeller, "Animal Instincts: 5 Ways Church Members Will Act in a Fight," Christianity Today, Winter 1993 Issue: Conflict, https://www.christianitytoday.com/pastors/1993/winter/93l1043.html.

8   Gottman, John, *The Science of Trust: Emotional Attunement for Couples* (New York: W.W. Norton & Co., 2011).

9   Gottman, John, *The Science of Trust: Emotional Attunement for Couples* (New York: W.W. Norton & Co., 2011), 142.

10  Boies, Jud, *Goals: Getting What You Want at Work and Home* (Granite Bay, CA: Business Goals Publishing, 2022).

11  Gottman, John, *The Science of Trust: Emotional Attunement for Couples* (New York: W.W. Norton & Co., 2011), 22.

12  Gottman, John, *The Science of Trust: Emotional Attunement for Couples* (New York: W.W. Norton & Co., 2011), 191.

13  Gottman, John, *The Science of Trust: Emotional Attunement for Couples* (New York: W.W. Norton & Co., 2011), 20–21.

14  Hax, Carolyn, "'Conversational narcissist' husband has something he'd like to add," Washington Post, May 21, 2021, https://www.washingtonpost.com/lifestyle/2021/05/22/carolyn-hax-husband-conversational-narcissist-happiness/.

15  Gregoire, Shelia Wray, *31 Days to Great Sex* (Grand Rapids: Zondervan, 2020), 21.

# ABOUT GIL STIEGLITZ

⸺ ∞∞∞ ⸺

D r. Gil Stieglitz is a prolific author, engaging speaker, and insightful pastor who has spent thousands of hours helping, coaching, and strengthening marriages. Gil has written over thirty books on marriage, parenting, soul development, and spiritual warfare, including top-seller *Becoming a Godly Husband, God's Radical Plan for Wives, Marital Intelligence, Building a Ridiculously Great Marriage, Mission Possible, Spiritual Disciplines of a C.H.R.I.S.T.I.A.N., Wise Parenting,* and *Touching the Face of God.* He speaks to thousands of people each year about the wonders of God's wisdom and principles. Gil serves as one of the Marriage and Family Life pastors at Bayside Church, a dynamic multi-site church near Sacramento, CA. He is the founder of Principles To Live By, a nonprofit organization that helps people connect to God's principles in everyday life. He and his wife, Dana, enjoy a ridiculously delightful marriage in Northern California. For more information about his other books and speaking, visit www.ptlb.com.

## Principles To Live By

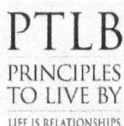

**PTLB**
PRINCIPLES
TO LIVE BY
LIFE IS RELATIONSHIPS

Principles To Live By is a 501(c)3 organization that equips and empowers people, pastors, and churches to build better relationships with God and each other. Our biblical resources magnify God and ignite hope for healthier marriages, families, spiritual lives, thriving churches, and vibrant communities. We hope to reach hundreds and thousands of people with God's principles for relational health. For more information, visit www.ptlb.com.

*To learn more about Gil and his books, resources, speaking, and consulting opportunities, visit www.ptlb.com.*

# MARRIAGE & PARENTING MATERIALS
## BY GIL STIEGLITZ

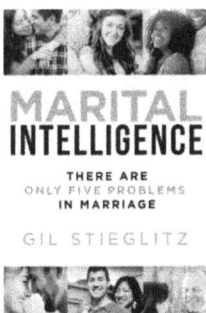

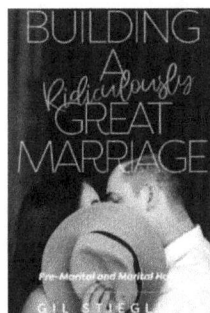

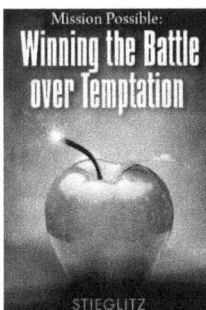

# MORE PTLB RESOURCES

Print Books

*Becoming a Godly Husband*

*Becoming Courageous*

*Breakfast with Solomon, Volumes 1–3*

*Breaking Satanic Bondage*

*Building a Ridiculously Great Marriage*

*Deep Happiness: Eight Secrets*

*Delighting in God*

*Delighting in Jesus*

*Developing a Christian Worldview*

*Getting God to Talk Back: Secrets of the Lord's Prayer*

*God's Radical Plan for Wives*

*God's Radical Plan for Wives Companion Bible Study by Jennifer Edwards*

*Going Deep in Prayer: Forty Days of In-Depth Prayer*

*Keeping Visitors*

*Leading a Thriving Ministry*

*Marital Intelligence: There Are Only Five Problems in Marriage (Reprinted 2019, BMH Books)*

*Mission Possible: Winning the Battle over Temptation*

*Proverbs: Devotional Commentary, Volumes 1–2*

*Satan and the Origin of Evil*

*Secrets of God's Armor*

*Spiritual Disciplines of a C.H.R.I.S.T.I.A.N.*

*The Gift of Seeing Angels and Demons: A Handbook for Discerners of Spirits by Susan Merritt*

*The Keys to Grapeness—Growing a Spirit-led Life*

*The Schemes of Satan*

*They Laughed When I Wrote Another Book about Prayer, Then They Read It*

*Touching the Face of God: Forty Days of Adoring God*

*Uniquely You: A Faith-Driven Journey to Your True Identity and Water Walking, Giant-Slaying, History-Making Destiny by Jenny Williamson*

*Weapons of Righteousness Study Guides*

*Wise Parenting: Creating the Joy of Family*

*Why There Has to Be a Hell*

## Audio Books

*Becoming a Godly Husband*

*Building a Ridiculously Great Marriage*

*Wise Parenting: Creating the Joy of Family*

Online Video Courses (Udemy.com)
Scan the QR code for more details.

How to Become a Good
and Godly Husband

Mission Possible:
Winning the Battle over
Temptation

The Keys to Grapeness—
Growing a Spirit-led Life

Spiritual Disciplines of a
C.H.R.I.S.T.I.A.N.

# PTLB

## PRINCIPLES
## TO LIVE BY

LIFE IS RELATIONSHIPS

PTLB.com